mantra

THE RULES OF İNDULGENCE

ecco

An Imprint of HarperCollinsPublishers

Jehangir Mehta

with CHRISTOPHER KELLY

Photographs by Bill Durgin

mantra

THE RULES OF INDULGENCE

This book is written as a source of information only. The information contained in this book should by no means be considered a substitute for the advice of a qualified medical professional, who should always be consulted before beginning any new diet, exercise, or other health program. The author and the publisher expressly disclaim responsibility for any adverse effects arising from the use or application of the information contained herein.

MANTRA. Copyright © 2008 by Jehangir Mehta. All rights reserved. Printed in the United States of America. No part of this book may be used or reproduced in any manner whatsoever without written permission except in the case of brief quotations embodied in critical articles and reviews. For information, address HarperCollins Publishers, 10 East 53rd Street, New York, NY 10022.

HarperCollins books may be purchased for educational, business, or sales promotional use. For information, please write: Special Markets Department, HarperCollins Publishers, 10 East 53rd Street, New York, NY 10022.

FIRST EDITION

Book design by Shubhani Sarkar

Library of Congress Cataloging-in-Publication Data is available upon request.

ISBN: 978-0-06-089985-1

08 09 10 11 12 ID/RRD 10 9 8 7 6 5 4 3 2 1

TO BALANCE, STRENGTH, LOVE, FAİTH, AND HOPE

Contents

mantra

THE RULES OF INDULGENCE

Introduction

THE CROWDED STREETS OF BOMBAY REGULARLY OVERFLOW WiTH festivals, and the roadside marketplaces leave a smell of spices hanging in the air. As a child growing up there, I was too close to the culture to notice most of its peculiarities, but I was always sensitive to the particular significance of food.

I wish I could start by telling you that at age fourteen I scrubbed the dishes at a French restaurant, and at age sixteen I slogged away in a kitchen—or, even better, that my grandmother and I cooked together for long hours in the kitchen. That was not the case.

We had cooks serving us at home. My mother and my sister, Firoza, absolutely detest cooking. And yet, on the rare occasions when she entered the kitchen, Mum dished out some incredible traditional fare, and I learned some very basic concepts: why dishes are made the way they are and what health benefits are provided by ingredients in the ayurvedic tradition.

According to common practice, each component of the typical diet has a specific effect on the body; therefore, food is a typical means of addressing many medical conditions. Walnuts, for instance, are eaten to alleviate backaches, and fennel promotes digestion. Fresh coconut water is consumed every day for its tremendous health benefits, as well as a spoonful of honey in warm water every morning and with a spoonful of cognac at night to fight a cold. Some foods are thought to have so many positive effects that their regular consumption is considered essential; these include avocado, honey, pomegranate, blueberries, and grapefruit.

Canned or prepared foods were almost unimaginable to me and were more expensive than fresh foods anyway. We drank fresh-squeezed orange juice. Milk was available in bottles, but I grew up drinking fresh milk, which had to be boiled every day and had a shelf life of just about two days. Fresh bread, fish, and eggs came to our doorstep daily. McDonald's was not in my vocabulary, and recycling was a way of life— a man came to our door and bought everything from newspapers to bottles to empty plastic pens.

This culture was governed by rules describing how and when certain foods should be eaten. These mantras needed to be followed at home and at school, and there were consequences for breaking them (on occasion, I was even caned in school). Not until years after I had left India did I learn to splurge and indulge my culinary whims—and of course, there is no better country than the United States to learn and practice splurging and indulging! This is the origin of the title *Mantra: The Rules of Indulgence*, which reflects the ayurvedic emphasis on balance: in this case, a balance of hot and cold, of Indian and American cultures and foods, of rules and indulgence. We all know that sugar and chocolate are not ideal nutritionally, but they simply need to be balanced with some fresh fruit. The aryuvedic principles and health benefits of many ingredients are described here just as they were instilled in me by my grandparents, parents, other relatives, and friends.

Although this background gave me an expansive historical perspective on food, I also wanted to build on the traditional identity of each ingredient to create a complete profile. By adopting other considerations, whether simple (taste, color, smell) or more complex (history, nutritional value, aesthetics), I wanted to reveal a much wider

range for most ingredients and find new, exciting applications that had never before been imagined.

Thus, when searching for a career, I decided to train as a chef. Although I was already well into my studies for a sociology degree at the University of Bombay, I enrolled in a four-year program at a hotel management school. I was soon convinced I had found the right path, and after graduation I moved to New York to study at the Culinary Institute of America (CIA).

The CIA gave me a broad set of new skills that transformed my unfocused passion for cooking into the disciplined work ethic that a restaurant kitchen would require. When I left school, my first job– a nine-month internship at L'Absinthe–offered me a chance to round out my remaining rough edges. From there, I joined the staff of Typhoon Brewery and worked under Patience Kamen and Eric Hubert. Six months later, Jean-Georges Vongerichten opened his namesake restaurant, and I took a second job working for him. Under this arrangement, I worked from eight AM until five PM at Typhoon Brewery, and then from five-thirty to midnight at Jean-Georges, seven days a week. Though exhausted by this schedule, I was committed to surviving it for at least a year. I was convinced that if I could withstand this kind of pressure, I would become a more seasoned and versatile chef.

I was rewarded for my dedication with the position of pastry chef at Mercer Kitchen, a new restaurant that Jean-Georges opened in SoHo, where I was allowed to design my own menu. I produced dishes that I knew would be crowd-pleasers: Roasted Figs Bathed in Port and Honey was an immediate hit, as was Sugar-Brushed Stone Fruit Bruschetta.

My Pineapple Cake was singled out in Ruth Reichl's review in the *New York Times* as epitomizing "the Mercer Kitchen at its very best." I stayed at Mercer Kitchen for a year and a half and then, during the whirlwind years that followed, worked in a number of restaurants including Union Pacific, Virot, Compass, Aix, and Sapa, and now my own restaurant, Graffiti.

Over the years, I became comfortable enough as a chef to return to my original focus on individual ingredients and my belief that these could be pushed beyond their traditional roles. I reached back to the past, drawing on the spices and herbs that I knew from childhood, to create dishes such as Fennel Ice Cream, Jasmine-Glazed Doughnuts, and Aloe Consommé. With each, I sought to demonstrate the unexpected range of ingredients, even in realms from which they had once been banished. Though most of these unusual plates were very well received, some aroused confusion and even scorn, particularly my Licorice Panna Cotta, Beet Sorbet, Salty Tapioca, and Vegetable Cake.

Because most of these experiments were successful, however, I was able to launch partistry.com, an event-management company plus online business that sells chocolates, confections, and teas, especially in exotic flavors, from around the world. My company has become known for its Kama Sutra chocolates, which are filled with herbed aphrodisiacs and painted with provocative images from the famous book. Partistry has also sponsored numerous cooking classes in New York kitchens, to spread an appreciation of essential flavors and reintroduce them outside the realm of desserts. In my new restaurant, Graffiti, I am able to give free rein to my ideas.

One of my good friends, Didier Virot, who is passionate about wine, would always summon me when he opened an interesting bottle: "J, come here if you do not want to die stupid." He would help me appreciate the fascinating aroma and flavors. This is the spirit that I want to embrace in this book.

Each recipe is accompanied by a brief description of the main ingredient so that you may come up with other, perhaps even more surprising, uses for it. You should also feel free to substitute ingredients: if a recipe calls for Thai basil, try it next time with a different kind of basil, or something else altogether. Be daring and experiment. And balance out the wickedness in your life!

FLOWERS

Lavender Citrus Tea

This deft blend of floral scents, sharpened with a tinge of citrus, is the perfect solution for both stress and fatigue.

20 SERVINGS

Combine the ingredients in a 2-cup airtight jar. You can store the tea in this jar for later use.

In a tea press, put 1½ tablespoons of the tea for every 10 ounces of boiling water you plan to add. Pour in the water. (If you are using a teapot, follow the same directions, but use a tea strainer when you pour the tea into a cup.)

Wait 4 minutes, and press.

½ cup dried lavender
   (see Suppliers List, page 197)
1 cup dried chamomile flowers
   (see Suppliers List, page 197)
⅓ cup dried orange peel, cut into
   small pieces
⅓ cup dried pineapple, cut into
   small pieces

LAVENDER exudes a pleasant, floral, almost pine-like aroma. It is often used in potpourris to scent houses. The flower originated in the Mediterranean region, and in ancient times, Romans would use lavender to scent the water of their baths; the word "lavender," in fact, is derived from the Italian *lavare*, to wash. Because of its rich aroma, lavender can be used very effectively to accent the flavors of soups and teas. English lavender has bluish-green leaves and blue-tinted buds, whereas French lavender has grayish-green leaves and dark purple flowers.

Cauliflower Clafoutis

6 SERVINGS

1 tablespoon sugar
1 whole egg (medium)
4 egg yolks (medium)
1½ cups milk
⅓ cup all-purpose flour, sifted
⅓ cup almond flour, sifted
  (see Suppliers List, page 197)
1 teaspoon kosher salt
5 tablespoons butter, melted
1 cup medium-size cauliflower
  florets

This dessert invigorates the classic clafoutis base with the sweetness of cauliflower, offering a unique interaction of old and new.

Preheat the oven to 325°F.

In a medium bowl, whisk together the sugar, egg, and egg yolks. Mix in the milk, flour, and almond flour. Whisk in the salt and butter. Stir in the cauliflower.

Pour into six 4-ounce ramekins. Place the ramekins in a baking dish and pour hot water around them. (The water level should reach about half the height of the ramekins.) Bake until the clafoutis set, about 15 minutes. Serve warm, in the ramekins.

CAULIFLOWER heads are composed of flower buds, albeit densely packed, underdeveloped ones. Although the exact history is unknown, it is thought that cauliflower first originated in the Mediterranean region and was then brought to the rest of Europe by explorers. The curds are usually white, although with some effort you can also find "broccoflower," a cross with broccoli that features a green curd and has a milder taste. There are even purple varieties as well. Cauliflower is very high in vitamin C, minerals, and fiber, and contains chemicals some believe can reduce the risk of cancer.

Vegetable Cake

Who knew that this classic blend of vegetables could make such a good dessert? You almost won't believe that this is good for you, or even that you're eating vegetables!

Preheat the oven to 350°F. Line a 10-by-4-by-4-inch loaf pan with parchment paper and spray with oil.

Bring a large pot of water to a boil. Separately blanch the cauliflower, artichokes, and broccoli for 1 minute each; remove with a slotted spoon or strainer and set in an ice bath. (This procedure partially cooks the vegetables while maintaining their firm texture.) Add the beets to the boiling water and cook for 5 minutes. Drain all the vegetables, place them in a bowl, and set aside.

Place the butter and sugar in the bowl of a standing mixer, and beat on high speed with a paddle attachment until the butter is fluffy and light, about 5 minutes.

Sift together the baking soda, flour, salt, and paprika. Turn the machine to low speed, and add the flour mixture and the eggs. Mix for 1 minute. Add the vegetables, raise the speed to medium, and mix for another 30 seconds.

Pour into the prepared pan and bake for 25 minutes, or until a toothpick pressed into the center of the cake comes out dry. When the cake is cool, remove it from the pan. Slice and serve, or store unsliced in an airtight box.

9 SERVINGS

1 cup medium-size cauliflower florets
5 fresh artichoke hearts, trimmed and cut into medium-size dice
1 cup medium-size broccoli florets
½ cup diced golden beets, cut small
½ pound (2 sticks) unsalted butter (not softened)
½ cup sugar
2¼ teaspoons baking soda
1 cup all-purpose flour
½ teaspoon kosher salt
½ teaspoon hot paprika
3 medium eggs

BROCCOLI, like its close relative the cauliflower, is part of the cabbage family. The first selection of sprouting broccoli originated in the regions of Greece and Italy. It is an excellent source of fiber and, in addition to being low in calories and fat, is thought by some to reduce heart disease and to contain anticarcinogens. Broccoli was widely used in ancient Rome and appears in Roman cookbooks served with cumin, coriander, and onion. America mostly uses green broccoli (calabrese), although purple and white varieties can also be found.

ARTICHOKES, with their elaborate architecture, can sometimes be intimidating, but the meaty, nutty flavor of the inner heart is well worth it. Though there are dozens of varieties around the world, nearly all the artichokes in the United States are the Italian green globe variety. Artichokes are thought to increase bile production and bile release in the liver. They have a high content of vitamin C, and are rich in fiber. When selecting an artichoke, look for the ones with the brightest and most tightly packed leaves.

Jasmine-Glazed Doughnuts

By brushing these sweet doughnuts with a mild floral glaze, one creates an intense, dynamic flavor that energizes the palate.

In a medium bowl, combine the yeast with the water and 2 cups of the flour. Cover with plastic and set aside in a warm place for 25 minutes.

Place the butter and sugar in the bowl of a standing mixer and beat at medium speed with a paddle attachment for about 5 minutes, until the butter is fluffy and light

Add the eggs, the salt, the remaining flour, and the yeast mixture, which should by now be bubbling. (If the mixture does not bubble, the yeast is dead, and you will need to start again with new yeast.)

Beat at medium speed until dough forms. (The dough has formed when it stops sticking to the sides of the bowl.) Remove the dough and, leaving it free-form, spray it with oil, cover it with plastic, and let it sit at room temperature for 1 hour to rise.

24 DOUGHNUTS

FOR THE DOUGHNUTS
1 ounce dry yeast
¾ cup lukewarm water
  (95°F to 110°F)
5 cups all-purpose flour
6 tablespoons (¾ stick) unsalted
  butter
⅔ cup sugar
4 medium eggs
Pinch of kosher salt

FOR THE GLAZE
½ cup dried jasmine flowers,
  (see Suppliers List, page 197)
¼ cup sugar

2 cups grapeseed oil, for frying

JASMINE flowers, native to Madagascar and the Comoros, have a sweet, intense scent often used in perfumes or incense. Many women in India use the flowers to perfume their hair. In Java, the flowers have a central role in wedding ceremonies and often adorn both the bride and the groom. As an ingredient, jasmine lends its essence well to teas, sauces, and oils. The scent, in addition to being pleasant to experience, is also thought to have sedative and calming properties.

For the jasmine glaze, combine the jasmine flowers, sugar, and ⅓ cup water in a saucepan. Stir over a low flame until the flowers are completely broken down, about 15 minutes. Strain into a small bowl and set aside.

Punch down the dough. Spread some flour on a countertop and roll out the dough ⅛-inch thick. Cut the dough into circles with a 2-inch round cookie cutter. Remove a ¼-inch circle from the center of each with another cookie cutter. Place the doughnuts on a nonstick baking sheet, spray with oil, and allow to rise again for 15 minutes.

While the doughnuts are rising, heat the oil to 350°F in a deep heavy pot.

Fry the doughnuts a few at a time until puffed and golden. Remove them with a slotted spoon and drain briefly on paper towels. While still warm, brush them on both sides with the jasmine glaze. Serve immediately.

Steamed Corn Pudding with Safflowers

5 ears fresh corn
4 medium eggs
½ cup heavy cream
½ teaspoon kosher salt
2 tablespoons unsalted butter,
 melted
1 tablespoon dried safflowers
 (see Suppliers List, page 197)
1 cup all-purpose flour
⅓ teaspoon freshly grated
 nutmeg
1 teaspoon baking powder
½ cup evaporated milk
½ cup sweetened condensed milk

This steamed pudding is reminiscent of traditional cornbread, but it is much more delicate and moist.

Spray twelve 4-ounce aluminum ramekins with oil.

Shuck the corn, and, using a chef's knife, cut the kernels off the cob.

Place the corn kernels, eggs, cream, salt, butter, safflowers, flour, nutmeg, and baking powder in a blender, and run until smooth, approximately 2 minutes. (The mixture should fit into a home blender; but if it does not, work in two batches.) Transfer to a large bowl, and add the evaporated and condensed milks. Using a spatula, reach down to the bottom of the bowl and gently fold the batter until all of the ingredients are incorporated and mixed together.

Pour the batter into the ramekins and set them in a steamer. Cover and steam for 20 to 30 minutes, until the puddings are springy. Serve warm in the ramekins, or unmolded onto a plate.

NOTES: To set up a steamer, bring a few inches of water to a boil in a wok, large pot, or deep skillet. Place a perforated pan, steamer basket, or metal rack on top, not touching the water. You could also use a rice cooker with a steaming attachment.

You can use 2 cups thawed frozen or drained canned corn if you don't have fresh corn.

{CONTINUED}

SAFFLOWER is known in some languages as "bastard saffron": though less expensive, the flower is no less brilliant in color, and it was long used as the base in some red and yellow dyes. Safflower is one of the oldest crops in human history, probably originating in the Mediterranean region, and its seeds were even found in King Tutankhamen's tomb. Its flowers offer little value as a spice, and are sometimes actually used to dilute saffron; the seeds, however, have a pronounced, slightly bitter taste. One can also extract from them oil that is believed to lower both cholesterol and blood pressure. It is rich in vitamin E and oleic acid.

Orange-Marigold Iced Tea

5 SERVINGS

⅓ cup sugar, optional
¾ cup fresh unsprayed, organic
   marigold petals (see Suppliers
   List, page 197)
3 tablespoons whole-leaf Assam
   tea (see Suppliers List,
   page 197)
2 oranges, well scrubbed

The cool taste of citrus and flowers make this iced tea divine for cooling down in the summer sun.

Bring 1 quart water (and the sugar, if using) to a boil in a medium saucepan. Add the marigold petals, reduce the heat, and simmer for 2 minutes.

Add the tea leaves, remove from the heat, and steep for 3 minutes.

Strain the liquid into a pitcher, discarding the marigold petals and tea leaves. Refrigerate until cold.

Slice the oranges into very thin discs. Line tall glasses with 5 to 7 slices each and pour in the cold tea.

MARIGOLDS are native to southern Europe and have dazzling yellow petals that instantly bring life to salads. Because of their intense color, the flowers were used for a long time to dye cheese. Marigolds are easy to grow and resistant to disease, so they can be cultivated around the world. Marigolds can be used to punctuate a wide variety of dishes, though they are most prominently showcased in teas and broths. The essence of marigold flowers is also thought to have anti-inflammatory properties.

Hibiscus Jamun (Baba)

The jamun—a spongy-textured ball-shaped cake like baba au rhum—simply melts in the mouth, releasing an intoxicating hibiscus perfume.

For the hibiscus syrup, combine the sugar and 3 cups water in a large saucepan and bring to a boil over a medium flame. Reduce the heat, add the flowers, and simmer for 25 minutes. Remove from the heat and allow to cool.

For the jamun, sift the flour and baking powder into the bowl of a standing mixer. Add the salt, powdered milk, and condensed milk. Beat with a paddle attachment on medium speed for 2 minutes or until dough forms. (The dough has formed when it no longer sticks to the side of the bowl.) Remove the bowl from the mixer, cover, and refrigerate for 10 minutes.

Heat the oil to 200°F in a deep heavy pot.

Tear off small pieces of dough and roll into balls about ¾ inch across. Fry about 4 pieces at a time, being sure to push the balls around in the oil so that all sides are evenly fried, about 7 minutes. Remove with a slotted spoon and drain on paper towels.

Add the balls to the hibiscus syrup, and steep for approximately 20 minutes. Spoon into a serving bowl. Serve with some syrup and hibiscus flowers.

12 JAMUNS, OR 12 SERVINGS

FOR THE HIBISCUS SYRUP
1 cup sugar
2 cups dried hibiscus flowers
  (see Suppliers List, page 197)

FOR THE JAMUN
½ cup all-purpose flour
½ teaspoon baking powder
Pinch of kosher salt
1 cup dry powdered milk
3 tablespoons sweetened
  condensed milk
1 quart grapeseed oil, for frying

HIBISCUS flowers exist in thousands of varieties, bearing brilliant hues of red, pink, purple, and yellow. Their broad variety is due at least in part to the ancient Chinese courts, which developed the native flower from its original form, thought to have been small and pink. Hibiscus teas were also a favorite of the Egyptian pharaohs. The petals lend an intense color to foods, and some recent studies have suggested that they can significantly reduce cholesterol levels.

Saffron-Glazed Nectarine Carpaccio with Yuzu Sherbet

4 SERVINGS

FOR THE GLAZE

½ gelatin sheet (for example, Kalustyan's; see Suppliers List, page 197)
½ teaspoon saffron threads
1 tablespoon sugar

FOR THE CARPACCIO

5 nectarines
6 apricots, pitted and diced medium

}See page 187 for the Yuzu Sherbet recipe. You will need about half the amount yielded there.{

This light, healthy dish is perfect for hot summer days. The saffron and fruit temper the tartness of the Yuzu Sherbet.

For the glaze, place the gelatin sheet in a bowl of cold water.

Combine the saffron, sugar, and ⅓ cup water in a small saucepan and bring to a boil. Reduce the heat and simmer for 5 minutes.

Remove the gelatin from the water and wring out extra liquid, as if from a towel. Stir the gelatin into the saffron mixture and whisk until it is dissolved. Set aside to cool.

For the carpaccio, slice the nectarines as thin as possible. Arrange one-quarter of the slices in a single layer in a circle about 10 inches across on a sheet of plastic wrap. Place a second sheet of plastic wrap over the circle. Create three more separate circles with the remaining nectarine slices.

Press a 9-inch ring mold onto the center of each nectarine circle. Using a paring knife, trim off the extra around the outside edge of the mold.

{CONTINUED}

Pick up a remaining inner circle and, resting it on your palm, gently remove the top sheet of plastic. Set a dinner plate upside down on top of the fruit. Invert the plate and fruit. Remove the other sheet of wrap. Repeat with the remaining fruit circles. Using a pastry brush, paint the nectarines with the saffron glaze.

Place a 2-inch ring mold in the center of the nectarines, and pack with the apricots. Gently remove the ring and set a scoop of yuzu sherbet on top. Serve immediately.

SAFFRON is the world's most expensive and revered spice, made from the dried stigmas (also called threads) of the saffron flower. More than ten thousand flowers are needed to create a single ounce of spice. Fortunately, only a bit of saffron is required to lend foods an intense yellow color; a pleasant, bitter taste; and a pungent, penetrating aroma. The spice is thought to have originated in Crete several thousand years ago. Historically, it was largely used as a spice and an herbal remedy, though it was also added to makeup, perfumes, and offerings. Threads have even been found sewn into ancient Persian rugs. Saffron is rich in vitamin B2 and riboflavin and is believed to have a calming effect on an upset stomach. Because the spice is so expensive and legendary, it is often adulterated. For this reason, it is always better to buy whole threads instead of powdered forms.

Chamomile Macaroons

The gentle scent of chamomile perfumes each bite of these sweet macaroons.

Preheat the oven to 275°F. Line a large baking sheet with parchment paper.

Sift together the confectioners' sugar and almond flour. Set aside.

Place ½ cup of the egg whites in the bowl of a standing mixer with a whisk attachment and beat at medium speed.

Combine the sugar and ⅓ cup water in a small saucepan over a high flame. Using a candy thermometer, measure the temperature. When the sugar water reaches 200°F, turn the mixer to high speed. (Continue to cook the sugar water.) Beat until the egg whites rise to a firm peak.

When the sugar water reaches 230°F, remove from the heat and pour slowly into the egg whites. Continue to beat until the bottom of the bowl cools to room temperature. Switch off the mixer, remove the whisk, and add the chamomile powder. Fold in gently, using a spatula.

Pour in the remaining egg whites (unbeaten) and gently fold them in. Add the sugar–almond flour mixture, reach down to the bottom of the bowl and fold the batter on top of itself until combined.

{CONTINUED}

12 MACAROONS

FOR THE MACAROONS
2 cups confectioners' sugar
2 cups almond flour
   (see Suppliers List, page 197)
¾ cup (5 to 6 large) egg whites
1½ cups sugar
1 teaspoon finely ground
   chamomile powder
   (such as Kalustyan's)

FOR THE CHOCOLATE GANACHE
2 cups heavy cream
1 tablespoon light corn syrup
½ cup dried chamomile flowers
   (see Suppliers List, page 197)
1 cup chopped dark chocolate
   (about 9 ounces)

Transfer the batter into a piping bag with a 1½-inch plain tip. Squeeze out 24 round discs, about 1½ inches across and ⅓ inch high, onto the prepared baking sheet.

Bake 12 to 15 minutes, until the macaroons feel dry to the touch. Set aside to cool, still on the paper.

In the meanwhile, prepare the ganache. Heat the cream and corn syrup in a saucepan over a high flame until hot. Whisk in the chamomile. Remove from the heat and steep for 5 minutes.

Place the chocolate in a medium heatproof bowl. Bring the cream mixture to a boil over a medium flame, remove from the heat, and slowly strain into the chocolate, whisking continuously. Keep whisking until the chocolate melts. Allow the ganache mixture to cool to room temperature. Transfer to a piping bag with a no. 2 plain tip, and refrigerate for 3 hours.

Pipe a ⅓-inch layer of ganache onto the back of one macaroon and top with a second macaroon, creating a sandwich with the ganache in the middle. Repeat with the remaining macaroons and ganache. Store in an airtight container for not more than 2 days.

CHAMOMILE flowers have a sweet, apple-like aroma; their name, in fact, is derived from the Greek *khamaimelon*, meaning "apple from the ground." During the Middle Ages, the flowers would be scattered on the ground during public events so that they would perfume the area when stepped on. The ancient Egyptians frequently used chamomile as a medicinal remedy and thought it a gift from the gods. Even today, chamomile is considered an excellent reliever of stress, muscle spasms, and menstrual cramps.

HONEY is the result of an evolutionary trick that attracts bees to flowers. The color and flavor of any particular honey depend on the flowers from which the bees extracted the nectar. Honey is an excellent natural sweetener, and it can be stored for long periods of time because it is resistant to bacteria and yeasts. The ancient Greeks discovered the healing properties of honey and used it to prevent infection. Honey is also useful when treating a sore throat, especially when combined with hot water and Cognac.

Chocolate Snack Bars with Foamed Honey Milk

6 SERVINGS

FOR THE CHOCOLATE BARS
1 cup chopped dark chocolate
   (about 9 ounces)
3 cups puffed rice
⅓ cup light raisins
⅓ cup dried cranberries
⅓ cup dried currants
⅓ cup crushed walnuts, cashews,
   or a mix

FOR THE HONEY MILK
1 quart milk
½ cup honey, such as acacia
   honey

These bars are great energy boosters and can be stored for several days in the freezer, so they are a good treat for a quick breakfast.

Melt the chocolate in a small bowl in the microwave. To ensure that it does not burn, check and stir it every 15 seconds until it is a smooth, warm liquid.

Line a baking sheet with parchment paper.

In a large bowl, stir together the melted chocolate and the puffed rice. Spread on the baking sheet until it is about ½ inch thick. Using another baking sheet of the same size, gently press down on the mixture to flatten it. Remove the top baking sheet.

Sprinkle with the fruits and nuts. Freeze for about 5 minutes, until the chocolate hardens.

Remove the pan from the freezer and, using a pizza cutter, cut into 6 individual bars of equal size. Freeze them in an airtight bag until they are to be eaten.

In a medium saucepan, combine the milk and the honey. Place over a high flame and whisk continuously to make it frothy. If you have a steamer, steam the milk with the honey. Pour into six tall heatproof glasses and serve with a chocolate bar.

Vanilla-Banana Flan with Raw Chocolate Sauce

The strong alcohol flavor and delicate texture of the flan are contrasted by the raw chocolate-caramel sauce drizzled around the plate.

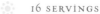 16 SERVINGS

FOR THE FLAN
1½ cups milk
1 vanilla bean
1¼ cups sweetened condensed milk
7 large egg yolks
¼ cup 99 Bananas Liquor, or any other banana liquor

FOR THE CHOCOLATE SAUCE
1 cup sugar
½ cup raw chocolate (rough-chopped cocoa nibs; see Suppliers List, page 197)

VANILLA BEANS come from the only orchid that produces edible fruit. The Aztecs had a long history of using the vanilla bean to flavor chocolate drinks, but not until the sixteenth century, when Cortez tasted it in a drink offered by Moctezuma II, was vanilla brought to Europe. Vanilla is expensive because it is difficult to obtain. When the vanilla fruit ripens and acquires its flavor, it opens and leaks out its contents; as a consequence, unripe fruits must be matured off the stem in a specialized process that takes several months. Vanilla has a sweet perfume and a smoky, woody flavor and it is believed to have relaxing properties.

Preheat the oven to 350°F and spray sixteen 2-ounce aluminum ramekins with oil.

Heat the milk in a medium saucepan over a medium flame until it begins to simmer. Split the vanilla bean lengthwise and scrape in the contents; also add the vanilla bean to the milk. Switch off the heat and, whisking continuously, add the condensed milk.

Whisk the egg yolks in a medium heatproof bowl. Continuing to whisk, pour in about half of the hot milk mixture. Pour the egg mixture back into the saucepan with the remaining hot milk. Stir in the banana liquor.

Strain into the ramekins. Place the ramekins in a baking dish and pour hot water around them. (The water level should reach about half the height of the ramekins.) Cover with foil and bake 20 minutes, or until set. Remove the flans and refrigerate.

For the sauce, melt the sugar in a medium saucepan over a medium flame. Once it begins to color, stir until it reaches a light gold. Add ¾ cup water and stir until the water has dissolved the caramel. Add the raw chocolate. Reduce the heat, simmer for 5 minutes, and transfer to a bowl to cool.

Unmold the flans onto plates, and serve with a drizzle of the raw chocolate sauce.

FRUİTS

VEGETABLES

ROOTS/
BULBOUS STALKS

RHİZOMES

Caraway Seed Cookies

This traditional Persian cookie offers a distinctive mix of sweet and spice that will leave a vivid impression on the tongue.

Preheat the oven to 300°F.

Sift the flour, salt, and baking powder into the bowl of a standing mixer fitted with a paddle attachment. Add the sugar and caraway seeds.

While beating on low speed, gradually add ½ cup water and the butter, alternating until both are completely incorporated. Continue to beat until the dough appears fairly smooth.

Roll the dough into 18 balls about 1 inch in diameter. Set the balls on a nonstick baking sheet and bake for 20 minutes. Rotate the baking sheet 90 degrees and reduce the temperature to 210°F. Bake 30 minutes more and rotate the sheet again. Bake another 30 minutes, or until the cookies are very light gold. Cool, and then store in an airtight box.

18 COOKIES

2 cups all-purpose flour
½ teaspoon kosher salt
1½ teaspoons baking powder
3 tablespoons sugar
1½ teaspoons crushed caraway seeds
6 tablespoons (¾ stick) unsalted butter, diced into small cubes

CARAWAY SEEDS are actually not seeds at all; they are fruits that grow from the blooming caraway plant. They have a pungent aroma and a somewhat sweet flavor that is unmistakable to anyone who has eaten rye bread. They probably originated in Asia and northern Europe and have been part of European cuisine for several centuries. The seeds have long been believed to prevent lovers and friends from straying, and they have sometimes been fed to homing pigeons to encourage their return.

Pear Beignets

1 tablespoon baking powder
1½ cups bread flour
Pinch of kosher salt
1 medium egg
1 cup Guinness stout
Grated zest of 1 orange
1 quart grapeseed oil
5 unpeeled, cored, cubed
   Bosc pears

Although this fried dessert may not be the healthiest way to consume fruit, it is certainly one of the best tasting.

Sift the baking powder, flour, and salt into a large bowl. In a medium bowl, whisk the egg, stout, and orange zest. Slowly pour the liquid into the flour mixture, and whisk until it forms a smooth paste.

In a deep heavy pot, heat the grapeseed oil over a medium flame until it reaches 350°F. Dredge 6 pear cubes at a time in the batter. Drop them one at a time into the oil and fry for 2 to 3 minutes, until they reach a light gold. Remove with a slotted spoon and drain on paper towels. Serve warm

NOTE: Make sure the pear cubes do not touch each other during frying, or they will stick together.

PEARS originated in the Caucasus and have been popular for thousands of years; the soft, delicious fruits that Homer called "a gift of the gods" are now nearly ubiquitous. The pear is high in fiber and contains vitamins that may lower high blood pressure and reduce the risk of stroke. It's also one of the sweetest fruits available, but it has very few calories. Pears come in thousands of varieties, and the most popular kinds include the Bartlett, Bosc, Forelle, Anjou, and Asian. The Bosc pear is especially good in desserts: its flesh is firmer than that of other varieties, and it retains its tall, crane-like appearance when cooked whole. The Bartlett pear, also known as the Williams pear, is the most popular, and often the only one available fresh during the summer.

Red Grape Sev

The Persians traditionally make a dish called sev on auspicious days. I like to combine it with red grapes for a juicier texture.

Heat the clarified butter in a medium sauté pan over a medium flame. Add the vermicelli and sauté about 7 minutes, until golden. Break the vermicelli into short lengths while sautéing.

Add the sugar and 2 cups water, cover the pan, and reduce the heat to low. Cook for about 10 minutes, until the vermicelli is al dente. Add more water if the vermicelli requires more time to cook but all the water has been absorbed. By the time the vermicelli is cooked, it should be dry.

Stir in the grapes and the almond essence or almond extract, and remove from the heat.

Pack the sev into 4 ring molds, each mold 3 inches wide by 1½ inches high. Invert the molds on dessert plates, then carefully remove the molds. Serve the sev warm.

4 SERVINGS

¼ cup clarified butter
  (see Suppliers List, page 197)
6 ounces vermicelli
3 tablespoons sugar
1 cup halved red seedless grapes
1 drop almond essence
  (see Suppliers List, page 197),
  or 1 drop almond extract

GRAPES were being cultivated as early as 6000 BC, and it is known that the Egyptians were producing wine soon thereafter. Several jars were even found in Tutankhamen's tomb, each bearing detailed information about the origin, vintner, and age. When grapes were brought to the Mediterranean, drinking wine became a true social pastime. The Greeks regularly consumed it at meals and social gatherings, though their crude, syrupy wine was typically diluted with water. The popularity of grapes today has depended in part on the development of table grapes, which are far less acidic than those used for wine. The skin of red grapes contains a chemical called resveratrol that has been shown to promote longevity, increase endurance, and combat inflammation.

Upside-Down Stone Fruit Bruschetta

4 SERVINGS

3 apricots

2 medium plums

1 nectarine

1 peach

3 kokums or 2 tablespoons
tamarind puree (the puree is
sold as tamarind paste;
see Suppliers List, page 197)

2 tablespoons sugar

½ teaspoon ground cinnamon

½ teaspoon freshly grated
nutmeg

1 vanilla bean

1½ cups panko (Japanese-style
bread crumbs)

8 tablespoons (1 stick) unsalted
butter, melted

Instead of using bread, this sweet and tart bruschetta uses panko bread crumbs, which crunch when toasted and result in a much lighter dessert.

Preheat the oven to 350°F.

Slice the apricots, plums, nectarine, and peach into eighths, and slice the kokums. Toss the fruits in a large bowl with the tamarind puree, if you are using it; the sugar; the cinnamon; and the nutmeg. Split the vanilla bean lengthwise and scrape in the contents. Toss again, and set aside for 10 minutes. (Note: You can put the empty vanilla pod into sugar or ground coffee, as a flavoring.)

In the meanwhile, soak the bread crumbs in the melted butter.

Divide the fruit into four 4-ounce ramekins and sprinkle with the bread crumbs.

Bake for 12 minutes, or until golden brown. Serve warm in the ramekins.

KOKUM is a dark purple plum from the *Garcinia indica* tree, found only in India. This sticky fruit is round and about 2 inches in diameter; once ripe, it is sun-dried, sometimes with salt. Because kokum is very cooling to the body, it can be diluted with water to create a refreshing beverage during the summer heat. In ayurvedic medicine, the fruit is thought to be an antihistamine, as well as a skin relaxant when the juices are topically applied.

Balsamic Figs with Grapes

 perfect hors d'oeuvre or side to a cheese course.

Preheat the oven to 300°F.

Crush the grapes by hand and place them in an oven-proof saucepan. Stir in the sugar and vinegar. Cook for 30 minutes over a medium flame, stirring occasionally, until a bit thick.

Add the figs. Bring to a simmer.

Cover the saucepan and transfer to the oven. Bake for 20 minutes, or until the figs are soft. Serve warm.

2 cups red seedless grapes
¼ cup sugar
⅓ cup balsamic vinegar
12 Black Mission figs, stemmed and sliced in half

FIGS pervade historical tales: they are specifically mentioned in the book of Genesis, in the account of the Garden of Eden; Romulus and Remus, the founders of Rome, were suckled by their foster mother, a wolf, while under a fig tree; Siddhartha was under a fig tree when he had a revelation that led to Buddhism; and the list goes on. In many countries figs are a symbol of fertility; in some countries, "making the fig," a gesture that involves inserting one's thumb between two fingers, is considered obscene. The Black Mission fig has light strawberry flesh and dark purple skin; the Calimyrna has pale pink flesh with yellowish green skin; the Kadota has amber flesh and green skin; and the Brown Turkey has light pink flesh and copper-colored skin. Figs are an excellent source of fiber.

Pineapple-Grape-Tarragon Salsa

4 SERVINGS

1 small fresh golden pineapple
Small bunch of red seedless
  grapes
2 sprigs of tarragon

Fresh fruit is incredibly invigorating when combined with freshly cut herbs. In this dish, the tarragon flavor nicely accents the pineapple and grapes.

Peel the pineapple and dice it into small cubes, avoiding the core. Cut the grapes into quarters.

Tear the leaves from the tarragon stems and chop into fine pieces.

Combine everything in a bowl and toss. Cover and refrigerate for about 30 minutes before serving.

PINEAPPLES are available year-round, and their rich, juicy flesh, whether raw or baked, is a popular addition to salads, yogurt, and pastries. There are several varieties, including the Baby Sugar Loaf, Del Monte Gold, Natal Queen, and Red Spanish. According to legend, the fruit originated in Brazil and the Caribbean, with Christopher Columbus bringing pineapples back to Europe after enjoying them on the island of Guadeloupe. The exotic shape and texture of the pineapple fascinated upper-class Europeans, who came to view it as a status symbol. Even in colonial America, fresh pineapples were sometimes placed at the center of a table as a symbol of hospitality. Because pineapples are rich in vitamin C, sailors would bring them on voyages to help prevent scurvy.

Palmyra Parfait

FOR THE PARFAIT

1 cup heavy cream

⅓ cup sugar

2 tablespoons light corn syrup

3 medium egg whites

1 cup fresh or canned peeled, diced small palmyra (such as Kalustyan's; see Suppliers List, page 197, but note that palmyra might be listed as palm fruit)

1 cup paillette feuilletine (see Suppliers List, page 197), or cornflakes or other flaked cereal

FOR THE CHOCOLATE PALMYRA

½ cup heavy cream

1 cup chopped milk chocolate (about 9 ounces)

1 cup canned peeled, diced small palmyra or fresh coconut

Eating cereal could not be made any better. If fresh palmyra is not available, purchase it canned.

For the parfait, whip the heavy cream to soft peaks. Cover and refrigerate.

Combine the sugar and corn syrup in a small saucepan over medium heat. Cook until it reaches 275°F on a candy thermometer.

In the meanwhile, place the egg whites in the clean bowl of a standing mixer with a clean whisk attachment. Whisk on high speed until the egg whites form stiff peaks and look firm.

Carefully pour the cooked sugar into the egg whites, and continue to whisk until the bottom of the bowl cools to room temperature. Switch off the mixer and remove the bowl and whisk.

Add the palmyra and the whipped cream to the egg whites. Reach down to the bottom of the bowl with a spatula and fold the mixture onto itself, until well incorporated.

Transfer to an airtight container and freeze for about 2 hours, until it sets.

{CONTINUED}

For the chocolate palmyra, in the meanwhile heat the cream in a small saucepan over a medium flame until it begins to boil. Place the chocolate in a medium heatproof bowl and pour the hot cream over it. Whisk until the chocolate is completely melted. Fold in the diced palmyra. Cool before plating.

Scoop 2 tablespoons of the chocolate palmyra into a martini glass, or wineglass, or dessert glass. (Not all of the mixture will be needed.) Flatten with a plastic disc or a spoon so it presses down perfectly. Add a large spoonful of the parfait and flatten it as well. Top it all with paillette feuilletine.

PALMYRA fruit goes by a few names, including palm fruit, palm seed, and lontar. The palmyra palm can grow up to 90 feet high, and its fruit resembles a small three-sided coconut, with a smooth, thin outer covering that turns black very soon after harvest. Within the fruit is the mature seed, a solid white kernel resembling coconut meat but much firmer. When the fruit is young it is soft and jelly-like, almost resembling ice, and oozes a sweetish, watery liquid when cut. By tapping the palm, one can harvest a sweet sap, called toddy, which ferments naturally within a few hours and is a very popular beverage. The palmyra that comes in cans is more mature than a fresh fruit. Palmyra is believed to be soothing to the body.

Grapefruit Three Ways

This dessert nicely showcases the various parts of the grapefruit, using the pith, the skin, and the flesh in three small dishes. This recipe can be used as a topping for ice creams, as a sauce for tarts, or as a breakfast marmalade.

10 SERVINGS

4 medium pink grapefruits
Sugar
2 cups freshly squeezed orange
 juice

For the candied grapefruit pith, bring a medium saucepan of water to a boil. Peel two of the grapefruits, leaving enough pith so that the skin with the pith is about ⅛ inch thick. Set the flesh aside in a bowl. Cut the skin into 2-by-1-inch rectangles and blanch them in the boiling water for about 2 minutes. Drain and repeat twice more. (Each blanching draws out some bitterness.)

Combine 2 cups sugar and 4 cups water in the saucepan and bring to a boil over a high flame. Add the blanched skins. Reduce the heat and simmer for about 1½ hours, until the skins are soft and sticky and the liquid has reduced almost completely. Drain the skins and set aside.

For the orange grapefruit skin, bring a medium saucepan of water to a boil. Carefully cut the skin off the remaining two grapefruits. (Add the flesh to the first two in the bowl.) Using a sharp knife, remove any remaining pith from the skin. Julienne the skin.

As above, blanch the skin in water three times to remove bitterness.

Combine 2 cups sugar and the orange juice in the saucepan and bring to a boil over a high flame. Reduce the heat to medium. Add the julienned skin. Simmer for about 20 minutes, until the skins are almost soft but still have a slight bite. Drain and set aside.

For the grapefruit marmalade, weigh the grapefruit flesh and measure an equal weight of sugar. Segment and seed the flesh. Transfer the pieces, along with any juice that may have been squeezed out of them, to a saucepan.

Add the sugar and bring to a boil, stirring, over a high flame. Reduce the heat to medium. Simmer for about 1½ hours, until thick.

Serve cool on a small plate. If you have any extra, it can be used as a sauce or a sweet topping for ice cream.

NOTE: You can refrigerate and store these components in airtight containers.

GRAPEFRUITS are a cross between a pomelo and an orange, and they were given the name because they grow in grape-like clusters on the tree. The "grapefruit diet" fad of the 1970s was not healthful or even effective, but grapefruit has been found to slow metabolism of certain drugs in the liver. The fruit also delivers a solid dose of vitamin C. When shopping for grapefruits, be aware that there are white, red, and pink varieties in the market, with varying levels of tartness.

Congolais (Coconut Macaroons)

Coconut macaroons, freshly baked, have an amazing aroma and a delicious, irresistible flavor.

☀ 4 DOZEN MACAROONS

9 medium eggs
4 cups desiccated coconut
  (see Suppliers List, page 197)
4 cups sugar
2 tablespoons vanilla paste
  (see Suppliers List, page 197)
⅓ cup chopped dark chocolate
  (about 3 ounces)
Toasted shredded fresh coconut,
  optional

Preheat the oven to 350°F. Line a baking sheet with parchment paper.

Place the eggs, desiccated coconut, sugar, and vanilla paste in the bowl of a standing mixer with a paddle attachment, and beat for 10 minutes at medium speed.

Roll out small balls of dough, about 1 inch in diameter, and place them on the prepared baking sheet. Pinch the sides of each ball with your forefinger and thumb to give it a slight oblong shape. Bake for approximately 5 minutes, until light golden brown.

While the congolais are baking, melt the chocolate in the microwave. To ensure it does not burn, check on and stir the chocolate every 15 seconds until it is smooth.

Drizzle chocolate over the top of the congolais. Let the chocolate cool and set at room temperature. Garnish the plate with lightly toasted coconut shreds, if desired.

COCONUTS, native to southern Asia, are the delicious fruits of the palm tree, and they lend themselves to a variety of culinary applications. Coconut milk gives a smooth, distinctive taste to sauces; dried coconut adds great flavor to pastries; and the sweet coconut water accessed by cracking through the shell is a refreshing and nutritious drink. Coconut oil is high in saturated fat, and has been advertised in some weight-loss programs as an alternative to oils rich in trans fats. Coconuts have three eyes, one of which caves in far more easily than the others, so when opening a coconut be sure to try each of them.

Green Papaya and Persimmon Salad with Pepper-Coconut Sorbet

6 SERVINGS

1 medium green papaya
2 ripe persimmons
1 teaspoon olive oil
Pinch of kosher salt
1 teaspoon sugar, optional
Microherbs, for garnish

{See page 186 for the
  Pepper-Coconut Sorbet recipe.}

The fresh, crisp taste of papaya offers a great textural counterpoint to the soft, gentle persimmon. A scoop of coconut sorbet makes this plate extremely cool.

Remove the skin from the papaya, using a peeler. Slice the fruit lengthwise into ⅛-inch slices using a mandoline or knife, and cut each slice into long juliennes (sticks). Place in a medium bowl.

Peel the persimmon and cut into thin slices. Add to the papaya.

Toss the papaya and persimmon with the olive oil and salt. (Adding sugar will help to break down the persimmon, but the sugar can be left out to reduce the level of sweetness.)

Arrange small bunches of the fruit in circular mounds on a plate. Place a scoop of sorbet on each. Garnish with microherbs.

PERSIMMONS are much more popular in Asia than in the United States. They come in two kinds, astringent and nonastringent. The astringent varieties are unbearably bitter until they become soft and ripe, at which point their flavor becomes sweet. Nonastringent persimmons do not have a bitter taste before ripening and can be eaten while still firm. The Hachiya is a heart-shaped astringent variety, whereas the Fuyu is nonastringent. The unique and captivating taste of persimmons has won them many fans and is absolutely worth sampling. Persimmons are thought to lower the risk of cardiovascular disease because of their antioxidant content.

Prune Muffins

Not only is this one healthful muffin—the taste of the prunes explodes when they are baked.

½ cup sugar
12 tablespoons (1½ sticks)
   unsalted butter
1 medium egg
½ teaspoon vanilla paste
   (see Suppliers List, page 197)
½ cup all-purpose flour, sifted
1 teaspoon baking soda
Pinch of kosher salt
⅓ cup sour cream
⅓ cup sliced pitted prunes

Preheat the oven to 350°F. Spray 20 mini muffin cups with oil.

Place the sugar and butter in the bowl of a standing mixer, and beat on high speed with a paddle attachment until the butter is fluffy and light, about 5 minutes. Add the egg and vanilla paste and mix for 1 minute.

Add the flour, baking soda, salt, and sour cream; mix for 20 seconds more. Add the prunes. Mix for 10 seconds. Remove the bowl and paddle and use a spatula to mix thoroughly. Spoon the batter into the muffin cups until each is three-quarters full.

Bake the muffins for about 12 minutes, or until golden brown. Allow them to cool before serving.

PRUNES are dried plums. It is believed that plums have been dried into prunes for thousands of years. There are many varieties of plums but only a few kinds of prunes, the most common ones being the Californian and French Agen. As plums shrink during the drying process and lose a considerable amount of water weight, their nutrients become more concentrated; as a result, prunes are dense in vitamins and fiber and are considered one of the most antioxidant-rich foods. Because sugar concentration increases during the drying process, prunes are also great for snacking.

Mint Sorbet with Candied Kumquats

7 SERVINGS

FOR THE SORBET
1 cup sugar
4 cups loosely packed mint leaves

FOR THE KUMQUATS
½ pound kumquats
4 cups sugar

This dish is extremely refreshing on hot summer days.

For the mint sorbet, combine the sugar with 2½ cups water in a medium saucepan and bring to a boil over a medium flame. Add the mint leaves and boil for about 1 minute. Remove from the heat and set in an ice bath to chill.

Transfer to a blender and puree at high speed. Process in an ice-cream machine according to the manufacturer's directions. Transfer to freezer.

For the kumquats, bring a large pot of water to a boil over a medium flame. Add the kumquats and boil for 2 minutes, then drain. Repeat this process three more times (each one draws some of the bitterness out of the kumquats).

Combine the sugar and 1½ quarts water in a clean medium saucepan and bring to a boil over a medium flame. Add the kumquats and simmer for 2 hours, or until they are soft and candied and the syrup is almost completely reduced.

Drain the kumquats and set aside on a sheet pan to cool. Once they reach room temperature, make a small hole in each and scoop out the seeds.

Serve the kumquats with a scoop of sorbet.

{CONTINUED}

KUMQUATS look just like citrus fruits and were originally categorized as such; indeed, their name roughly means "golden orange" in Chinese. Unlike oranges, however, kumquats have a sweet skin that is usually eaten along with the fruit. The fruits have become popular bases for jellies and syrups and are available fresh at markets throughout winter. Meiwa kumquats are round, sweet, and large; Nagami are oval and yellow; and Marumi are round and golden. Kumquats are a good source of vitamin C and citric acid.

Copra Pak (Coconut Compote)

4 SERVINGS

1 medium dried coconut, grated
  (see Suppliers List, page 197),
  or 1½ cups desiccated coconut
1 cup sugar
3 cups evaporated milk
2 cups dried goji berries
  (see Suppliers List, page 197)
1 vanilla bean

Back in India, my aunts Naju and Arnu taught me how to make this authentic dish. There are slight variations in my version, but this dish always brings back memories of home.

Place the coconut, sugar, milk, and berries in a large saucepan. Split the vanilla bean lengthwise and scrape in the contents. (Note: The empty vanilla pod can be put in a jar with sugar, to make vanilla sugar for future use.) Over a medium flame, stir almost continuously until the milk dries out and the oils of the coconut emerge, about 45 minutes. (By the end, the oils from the coconut should leak out, causing the mixture to slide around rather easily.)

Transfer to a bowl and serve warm.

GOJI berries are sweet, scarlet red dried fruits about the size and texture of a raisin. They are grown in Tibet and in the Himalayas. The berries are traditionally considered to boost one's strength and immune system. According to a popular myth, a man lived to the age of 252 just by eating goji berries daily. Despite such exaggerations, the berries do have some medicinal value and can be found at health stores.

Cranberry Scones

You can drive the British out of India, but you can't take their scones out of Indian teatime. These are great pastries, especially when they first come out of the oven.

15 SCONES

3½ cups bread flour
½ cup sugar, plus additional
   for sprinkling
½ teaspoon kosher salt
½ pound (2 sticks) unsalted
   butter, cut into 1-tablespoon
   pieces
⅓ cup heavy cream
4 medium eggs
½ cup dried cranberries
   (if necessary, refresh these in a
   little hot water)
1 tablespoon baking powder

Preheat the oven to 325°F.

Place the flour, sugar, salt, and butter in the bowl of a standing mixer with a paddle attachment and beat on medium-high speed until all of the ingredients are mixed, about 5 minutes. Add the cream, eggs, cranberries, and baking powder. Beat for about 30 seconds more. Then turn the switch off. Don't overmix! Less mixing is better than too much.

On a floured surface, roll out the dough to a 5-by-3-inch rectangle about 1 inch thick, and with a sharp knife cut into 1-inch cubes.

Place the cubes on a nonstick baking sheet, sprinkle with sugar, and bake until light gold, about 10 minutes. Allow to cool slightly and serve warm; or cool more and serve at room temperature.

CRANBERRIES are tart berries that originated in the Americas. Cranberry juice is popular but is loaded with sugar to offset the tartness. Though white cranberry juice is also common, there is no such thing as a "white cranberry"–the berries are simply pressed a few weeks earlier than usual, before they turn red. Cranberries have a long shelf life because of their waxy skin, which contains a natural preservative. They are rich in antioxidants and can decrease levels of LDLs, the so-called bad cholesterol.

Guava-Tamarind Brittle

6 SERVINGS

1 cup guava paste
   (see Suppliers List, page 197)
⅓ cup tamarind paste or
   tamarind concentrate
   (see Suppliers List, page 197)
⅓ cup raisins
½ cup pine nuts
Manchego cheese (or any hard
   Spanish cheese, or Italian
   Piave) and bread, for serving

This brittle, also called chikki, is similar to a sticky, chewy toffee. It was popular among my classmates when I was growing up in India.

Preheat the oven to 275°F.

In a bowl, mash together the guava paste and 1 tablespoon hot water until smooth. Stir in the tamarind paste or concentrate. Add the raisins and pine nuts and stir until well incorporated.

Pour onto a nonstick baking mat. Place another mat on top. Press the top mat with a rolling pin to flatten and spread the mixture, until it is as flat and thin as possible.

Remove the top mat and place the mat with the brittle on a baking sheet. Bake for 30 minutes, or until the brittle feels dry to the touch. Remove from the oven and set aside to cool. Tear off pieces after it comes to room temperature. Serve with Manchego cheese (or another cheese, as noted above) and bread.

{CONTINUED}

TAMARIND is a thick brown fruit native to tropical Africa, although it has been cultivated in India for so long that most of its history resides there. There is a popular myth that Lord Krishna sat under a tamarind tree while pining for his lover Radha. Even the name is derived from the Arabic *tamr hindi*, which means "Indian date," a presumed reference to the tamarind's date-like appearance when dried. The sour, piquant taste of the young tamarind is not particularly popular in American cuisine, though many Americans have experienced it in Worcestershire sauce. In traditional ayurvedic medicine, tamarind is used to promote digestion.

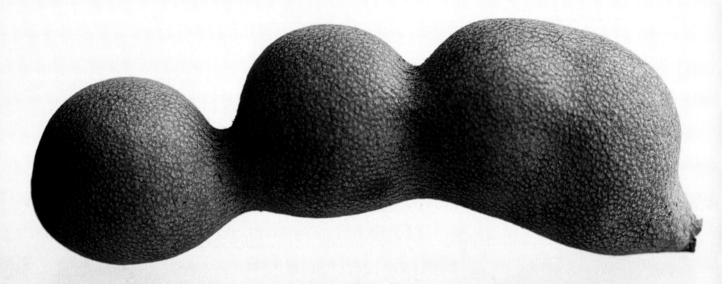

Yogurt Pancakes with Rhubarb Compote

4 SERVINGS

FOR THE COMPOTE

1 pound rhubarb, peeled and
   chopped into small, even pieces
½ cup sugar
½ cup strawberry puree
   (see Suppliers List, page 197),
   or make your own as noted
   below, using an additional ½
   pound of strawberries
3 tablespoons balsamic vinegar

FOR THE PANCAKES

4 medium egg whites
2 tablespoons sugar
½ cup unflavored yogurt
2 tablespoons all-purpose flour,
   sifted
2 turns of black pepper from
   a mill

Fresh pancakes topped with tart rhubarb is a delightful combination, as well as a fun, colorful breakfast.

NOTE: If the strawberry puree specified in the ingredients list is unavailable, you can make your own by mashing an additional ½ pound of strawberries in a food processor and then reducing the puree, over medium heat, to ½ cup.

For the compote, combine the rhubarb, sugar, strawberry puree, and vinegar in a medium saucepan. Bring to a simmer over a medium flame. Cook, stirring occasionally, until it becomes thick, about 45 minutes. Transfer to a bowl, cover with plastic, and cool in the refrigerator.

{CONTINUED}

For the pancakes, preheat the oven to 325°F.

Place the egg whites in the bowl of a standing mixer with a whisk attachment and whisk until frothy, 2 to 3 minutes. Add the sugar, and continue to whisk until the egg whites are medium-bodied and able to remain in a peak-like shape on the inverted whisk.

In a large bowl, whisk together the yogurt, flour, and pepper until completely mixed.

Using a spatula, gently place about one-third of the whipped egg whites on top of the yogurt, reach down to the bottom of the bowl and fold the yogurt on top of the egg whites, continuing until the two are mixed. Repeat with the remaining egg whites.

Spray a large nonstick frying pan with oil and heat over a medium flame. Scoop out large tablespoons of the batter to form small pancakes. Cook about 30 seconds on each side, or until they are a very light golden. Transfer the pancakes to a nonstick baking sheet as they are done. Continue until all the batter has been used, spraying the pan again if necessary.

Place the baking sheet in the oven and heat the pancakes for about 1 minute. Serve immediately with the cold rhubarb compote.

RHUBARB was a medicine long before it was a food, and for thousands of years the Chinese gave rhubarb as a laxative without much thought for its culinary value. A member of the buckwheat family, rhubarb is actually a vegetable, although it is generally thought of as a fruit. Though the leaves are known to be toxic, they are harmless in small quantities. There are two basic types of rhubarb: hothouse, also known as strawberry rhubarb, has a delicate texture and smooth flesh, but cherry rhubarb is juicier and more acidic and has a deeper color.

Cucumber Water

This is a refreshing beverage to drink in the sauna, with the taste of cucumber exerting a cooling effect on the body.

ABOUT I QUART

Two 12-inch unpeeled cucumbers
   (with seeds), julienned
½ teaspoon kosher salt
½ lemon

Add the cucumbers and salt to 1 quart water in a pitcher. Squeeze in the lemon juice and drop in the squeezed lemon.

Briefly stir. Cover and refrigerate until cold. Remove the lemon shell. Strain before drinking, if you prefer.

CUCUMBERS are native to India and come in several varieties. The garden cucumber is the most common, though the others (including Armenian, lemon, Japanese, Kirby, hothouse, and English) are worth looking for. Cucumber sandwiches are a popular snack at cricket matches in India, where they play the same role as hot dogs at baseball games in America. Cucumber slices are more than 90 percent water and, as a result, are often sometimes placed over the eyes to increase hydration. The cucumber is also thought to be useful for lowering blood pressure and promoting digestion.

Lime-Brushed Melon Mille-Feuille with Beet Sorbet

This elegant stack of melon and citrus, topped with beet sorbet, is one of the healthiest desserts in this book.

For the beet sorbet, boil the beets in 1 quart water over a medium flame until they are easily pierced with a knife, about 45 minutes. Drain the beets and cool in an ice bath.

The final plate will be garnished with small cubes of beet. Peel and small-dice half of one beet, and reserve, covered, in the refrigerator. Peel and coarsely chop the rest of the beets.

Place the chopped beets, sugar, and 2 cups water in a blender and puree until liquefied. Process in an ice-cream machine, according to the manufacturer's directions, and store in the freezer.

For the lime jus, place the gelatin in a bowl of cold water.

When the gelatin sheets resembles a limp towel, remove them from the water and wring out excess liquid. Place in a medium bowl.

4 SERVINGS

FOR THE SORBET
5 medium beets
½ cup superfine sugar

FOR THE LİME JUS
2 gelatin sheets
   (see Suppliers List, page 197)
10 fresh Kaffir lime leaves
   (see Suppliers List, page 197)
3 tablespoons sugar

1 honeydew melon
Assorted microherbs, for garnish
   (see Suppliers List, page 197)

{CONTINUED}

Place the lime leaves, sugar, and 1 cup water in a medium saucepan and bring to a boil over a medium flame. Reduce the heat and simmer for 10 minutes. Strain the liquid into the bowl with the gelatin. Whisk until the gelatin has dissolved. Set the bowl in an ice bath to cool until syrupy.

Peel the melon and cut it into ⅛-inch-thick semicircular slices. Place the slices in one layer on a baking sheet. Using a pastry brush, coat each slice with a thin layer of lime jus.

To create the mille-feuille, stack the melon slices in two adjacent stacks on a dessert plate, interleaving the slices slightly at first but more so as the stacks get higher, they form a pyramid. Stack 8 or 10 slices. Repeat on three other plates. The stacks must be able to bear the weight of a scoop of sorbet.

Swirl some lime jus over each plate, and scatter the diced beets and microherbs as garnish. Carefully top each melon stack with a scoop of sorbet.

BEETS are a sweet, firm root, delicious raw or cooked. The rich red color of the standard beet is so pronounced that it was sometimes extracted to dye other foods, though white and golden beets can also be found. There is even a red-and-white-striped variety called the chioggia. Though beets contain more sugar than any other vegetable, they are also potent sources of folic acid and vitamins A and C. They are also surprisingly low in calories. The ancient cookbook *The Art of Cooking* features, as laxatives, several soups containing beets.

Carrot Cake

12 SERVINGS

 Candied strands of carrot add an exciting texture to this variation on the traditional carrot cake.

FOR THE GARNISH

2 cups sugar

2 whole star anise

1 cinnamon stick, about 3 inches long

1 cup julienne carrots (preferably supermarket carrots or farmers' market carrots)

FOR THE CAKE

2 cups light brown sugar

8 tablespoons (1 stick) unsalted butter

5 medium eggs

¾ cup milk

1 tablespoon ground allspice

1 tablespoon ground cinnamon

1½ teaspoons ground star anise (to make your own, fine-grind 2 whole star anise in a spice grinder)

4 teaspoons baking soda, sifted

2 cups all-purpose flour, sifted

4 cups grated carrots (about 1¾ pounds, trimmed)

¼ cup diced unsalted pistachios, lightly toasted and chopped (optional)

For the garnish, bring the sugar and 2 cups water to a boil in a medium saucepan over a high flame. Reduce the heat and mix in the star anise, cinnamon, and carrots. Simmer for about 45 minutes, stirring occasionally, until the carrots are soft and sticky.

Remove the carrots with a slotted spoon and set aside in a bowl. Discard the cinnamon, the star anise, and any liquid that is left.

{CONTINUED}

Preheat the oven to 350°F.

For the cake, place the brown sugar and butter in the bowl of a standing mixer with a paddle attachment, and beat at medium speed until the butter is light and fluffy, about 5 minutes.

Add one egg at a time, making sure each is completely incorporated before adding the next. While the mixer continues to run, add the milk, spices, baking soda, and flour.

Remove the bowl from the mixer and add the grated carrots. Using a spatula, reach down to the bottom of the bowl, and fold the batter onto itself until the carrots are completely incorporated.

Pour the batter into 12 buttered individual rings, each 2 inches in diameter by 3 inches tall. The rings will be about three-quarters full. Bake for 15 to 18 minutes, until a toothpick pressed into the center of the cake comes out dry.

Remove the rings and let the cake cool a bit; however, it should be served warm.

Place the candied carrot on top of cake. The chopped pistachios also add a nice texture and can be used as an optional garnish.

If the cake is not to be served right away, store it in an airtight box, and keep the candied carrots in a separate container.

CARROTS are perhaps the most widely eaten roots; whether juiced, raw, cooked, or whole, they are a staple of diets worldwide. Though orange carrots are predominant, carrots have also been bred to appear purple, yellow, red, and white. In fact, the original carrots, grown in Asia and the Middle East, were purple; the orange variety did not become popular until Europeans cultivated it in the 1600s to honor the royal house of Orange. The carrots we eat are rich in vitamin A, which is derived from the breakdown of the orange pigment, and can help fight cardiovascular disease. They also contain far more sugar than most other vegetables, and perhaps this explains their popularity as a quick snack.

Radish-Gourd Chutney

This chutney is a traditional dish from my childhood. Eat it with flatbread for a satisfying and healthy snack. White gourd, or white pumpkin, is light green on the outside but pure white inside.

Peel and grate the radish and white pumpkin.

Place the radish, pumpkin, sugar, salt, cinnamon, mace, and lime juice in a large saucepan and cook over a medium flame 40 to 50 minutes, stirring every few minutes, until all of the liquid boils off. The mixture should become thick, sticky, and golden.

Cool slightly, and serve in a small bowl. The chutney can be stored in an airtight jar in a cool, dry place.

2 CUPS CHUTNEY

1 pound small red radishes

1 pound white pumpkin, or white gourd (a 1-pound can of yellow pumpkin can be substituted, although this may alter the taste)

4 cups sugar

1½ teaspoons kosher salt

2 cinnamon sticks, each about 3 inches long

5 blades of mace, or ½ teaspoon ground mace

1 cup freshly squeezed lime juice

RADISHES probably originated in China, where they have been cultivated for several thousand years. In Greece, the root was so well liked that replicas were cast in gold and offered to the gods. The most popular variety is small and red, but the long white Japanese daikon radish is becoming more popular. Other varieties are pink, white, or black, and some can grow to the size of a soccer ball. Indeed, in preparation for the Night of the Radishes, an annual festival in Oaxaca, Mexico, that occurs right before Christmas, farmers carve their largest radishes into religious figures and re-create scenes from the birth of Jesus. The peppery flesh of radishes lends a great accent to salads and soups. Radishes are also rich in vitamin C and can help stimulate the appetite.

Licorice Panna Cotta
with Tangerine-Star Anise Tartare

Eric Asimov of the New York Times *specifically mentioned this item when discussing the more daring offerings of pastry menus. He wrote "A small circle of smooth, light and silky custard, it is deeply imbued with the warm, intense flavor of licorice, which lingers only if you avoid its accompanying pile of tangerine sections. Take a bite of the citrus and it stops the licorice flavor short; alternate bites and you have a captivating tennis match in the mouth."*

FOR THE TANGERINE-
STAR ANISE TARTARE

5 tangerines or clementines, peeled, segmented, and seeded

½ teaspoon ground star anise (to make your own, fine-grind 1 whole star anise in a spice grinder)

FOR THE CITRUS SAUCE

1 gelatin sheet
  (see Suppliers List, page 197)

½ cup freshly squeezed lemon juice

2 tablespoons sugar

⅓ teaspoon, or 5 drops, orange oil (see Suppliers List, page 197); to get drops, use a pipette or a squeezable bottle

FOR THE PANNA COTTA

1½ cups heavy cream

½ cup milk

½ cup sugar

2 tablespoons licorice powder
  (see Suppliers List, page 197)

1½ gelatin sheets
  (see Suppliers List, page 197)

Microherbs and ground star anise, for garnish
  (see Suppliers List, page 197)

{CONTINUED}

For the tartare, combine the tangerine segments and star anise in a bowl, cover, and refrigerate until chilled.

For the citrus sauce, place the gelatin sheet in a bowl of cold water. In a small saucepan over a medium flame, warm the lemon juice and sugar until the sugar is dissolved. When the gelatin sheet resembles a limp towel, remove it from the water and wring out the excess liquid. Stir the gelatin into the lemon juice until dissolved. Stir in the orange oil and remove from the heat. Transfer the sauce to a small bowl, cover, and refrigerate.

For the panna cotta, combine the cream, milk, and sugar in a medium saucepan over a high flame. When the mixture comes to a simmer, whisk in the licorice powder. Remove from the heat and steep for at least 30 minutes.

LICORICE, a dark brown, wrinkled root with a yellowish interior, is native to Asia and the Mediterranean. Its distinctive sweet taste is most often used to mask other, more unpleasant ones. In fact, the vast majority of licorice is used to sweeten medicines, cigarettes, and soft drinks, although licorice candy itself is popular worldwide. Licorice is thought to be excellent for one's health; in China it is the second-most prescribed ingredient in herbal medications, after ginseng. In the *Kama Sutra*, it is featured in many recipes that claim to increase sexual vigor. It is also believed to provide relief from a sore throat.

While the licorice is steeping, place the gelatin sheets in a bowl of cold water. When the gelatin sheets resemble a limp towel, remove them from the water and wring out the excess liquid. Bring the licorice-milk mixture back to a boil, add the gelatin, and switch off the heat. Whisk until the gelatin is completely dissolved. Place the saucepan in an ice bath. Stir occasionally as it cools until syrupy but not set.

Pour into eight 2-ounce ramekins. Refrigerate until set, about 3 hours.

To serve, place each ramekin on a plate. On the side, form the tartare by packing a 2-inch ring mold with the tangerines, then carefully removing the mold. Garnish the tartare with microherbs, a drizzle of the citrus sauce, and a sprinkle of ground star anise.

Chicory Soufflé

Here the strong aroma of chicory reaches even higher than the soufflé itself. I urge everyone to try making this recipe–if for nothing else, to discover that soufflés aren't as difficult as the myths would have us believe.

Bring the milk to a boil in a medium saucepan over a high flame. Switch off the heat.

Sift the cornstarch, ⅓ cup of the sugar, and the chicory into a small bowl. Whisk in the egg and yolk. Continuing to whisk, slowly add about half of the hot milk. Pour the mixture back into the saucepan with the remaining hot milk.

Cook over a medium flame, whisking continuously, until it begins to bubble. Reduce the heat and cook for 1 minute more, continuing to whisk.

Remove from the heat and pour into a bowl. Cover with plastic, pressing the plastic down into the bowl so it touches the surface. (This will prevent a skin from forming.) Set aside and cool to room temperature.

Once it has cooled, whisk in the Kahlúa. Re-cover the bowl with plastic as above. This will serve as the base for the soufflé.

Preheat the oven to 375°F. Set aside ¼ cup of the sugar.

9 SOUFFLÉS

2 cups milk
⅓ cup cornstarch
1 cup sugar
2 tablespoons ground chicory
   (see Suppliers List, page 197)
1 medium whole egg
1 medium egg yolk
2 tablespoons Kahlúa
Softened butter
7 medium egg whites

{CONTINUED}

Turmeric Yorkshire Pudding

16 SERVINGS

1 cup milk
8 tablespoons (1 stick) unsalted
   butter, melted
15 medium eggs
Pinch of kosher salt
3½ cups all-purpose flour
1 teaspoon ground turmeric
¾ cup duck fat (see Suppliers
   List, page 197)

The earthiness of tumeric lends an Indian flair to this otherwise traditional English dish.

In a large bowl, whisk together the milk, butter, eggs, salt, and 1 cup water. Sift the flour and turmeric onto the batter and whisk until combined.

Cover the bowl with plastic and let it rest at room temperature for about 30 minutes.

Preheat the oven to 475°F.

Set sixteen 4-ounce aluminum ramekins on a baking sheet, and place 1 tablespoon of duck fat in each. Place the ramekins in the oven for 5 minutes, or until the fat begins to smoke.

Remove the baking sheet from the oven and carefully ladle the batter into each ramekin until about halfway full. Bake for about 10 minutes, or until the puddings are puffed and golden brown. Remove from the ramekins while hot, and serve hot.

{CONTINUED}

TURMERIC was probably first cultivated in India, where it quickly assumed a major role in ayurvedic medicine. Current research has suggested that its active ingredient, curcumin, can indeed fight diseases such as cancer, heart disease, and Alzheimer's disease. As a child in India, I was told to eat a teaspoon of turmeric and sugar when I fell and hurt myself, as this mixture was thought to promote healing. In the kitchen, turmeric is known for the bright yellow color it adds to foods; this property earned it the nickname "Indian saffron." (Though it is less expensive than saffron, its somewhat pungent bitter taste usually makes it an inappropriate substitute.) Turmeric is almost always included in curry powders and is also a great addition to rice dishes, dressings, and soups. It can be purchased fresh or dried. Fresh turmeric is more aromatic but also milder than the dried form, which is earthier and slightly bitter. There are two main types of turmeric: the light yellow Madras variety, and the darker and earthier Alleppey variety.

LEAVES

HERBS

SPİCES

Tres Leches Cake with
Coconut-Curry Emulsion, Pears, and Almonds

*My sous chef Andres Vazquez taught me this
traditional Mexican dessert. I couldn't help but add
a small Indian flair with the curry emulsion, which
the cake absorbs quite well.*

12 SERVINGS

FOR THE CAKE
5 medium eggs
½ cup granulated sugar
½ cup all-purpose flour, sifted

FOR THE SOAKING LIQUID
1 cup sweetened condensed milk
½ cup evaporated milk
1 cup coconut milk
⅓ cup Malibu rum or other
   coconut-flavored rum

FOR THE PEARS AND ALMONDS
2 medium-size pears (such as
   Anjou, but any variety will do)
Juice of 1 lime
3 tablespoons unsalted butter
⅓ cup dark brown sugar
1 cup unsalted Marcona almonds
   (see Suppliers List, page 197)

FOR THE COCONUT-CURRY
EMULSION
⅓ cup heavy cream
2 tablespoons sugar
2 sprigs of fresh curry leaves
   (see Suppliers List, page 197)
½ cup coconut milk
⅓ cup pineapple juice

For the cake, preheat the oven to 350°F and line an 18-by-13–
by-1-inch jelly roll pan with parchment paper.

Using a standing mixer with the whisk attachment,
beat the eggs on high speed about 3 minutes, until they
are thick and foamy. Add the sugar and beat for another
10 minutes, until fluffy.

{CONTINUED}

Reduce the speed to medium and add the flour. Beat for 1 minute more. Switch off and remove the bowl from the mixer.

Using a spatula, reach down to the bottom of the bowl and gently fold the batter onto itself several times, until all of the flour is incorporated.

Gently spread the batter in the prepared pan, cover with foil, and bake for 30 minutes. Remove the foil and check the cake with a toothpick; if the center is still wet, cover again and bake until the center is set.

Let the cake, in the pan, cool to room temperature. Still leaving it in the pan, wrap it in plastic and refrigerate until chilled.

For the soaking liquid, in a medium bowl, combine the condensed, evaporated, and coconut milks with the rum. Pour evenly over the cake, and let soak overnight in the refrigerator.

For the pears and almonds, peel and core the pears. Use a melon baller to remove balls of flesh. Place the pear balls in a small bowl and sprinkle with the lime juice.

Melt the butter in a small sauté pan over a medium flame. Add the brown sugar. When the brown sugar has dissolved, add the pear balls. Toss over a high flame for 2 minutes. Mix in the almonds, remove from the heat, and cool to room temperature. Set aside.

For the coconut-curry emulsion, heat the cream and sugar in a small saucepan until almost boiling. Add the curry leaves, switch off the heat, and steep for 20 minutes. Strain the cream into a medium bowl. Mix in the coconut milk and pineapple juice, and whisk until the mixture becomes slightly frothy.

Cut the cake into 12 squares, pour the emulsion over them, and serve them garnished with the almonds and pears.

CURRY LEAVES are intoxicatingly fragrant but fleetingly so: after only a few days, the leaves dry up and lose most of their smell. As a consequence, they must always be purchased fresh. The leaves are smaller than lemon leaves but carry a shine. Curry leaves are native to India and are a staple ingredient in South Indian and Sri Lankan cuisine, where they are used either fresh or lightly cooked in oil. In India, curry leaves are also eaten to control diabetes.

Verbena-Chocolate Tart

6 TARTS

FOR THE GARNISH
1 cup sugar
50 fresh verbena leaves (see Sup-
    pliers List, page 197)

FOR THE SAUCE
1½ cups sugar
4 fresh betel leaves, chopped fine
    (see Suppliers List, page 197)

FOR THE VERBENA-CHOCOLATE
GANACHE
1½ cups heavy cream
2 tablespoons light corn syrup
15 fresh verbena leaves
    (see Suppliers List, page 197)
1 cup chopped bittersweet
    chocolate (about 9 ounces)
2 tablespoons unsalted butter,
    diced

*The combination of chocolate and verbena is divine.
This dessert must be tasted to be believed.*

NOTE: Because tart shells tend to break while baking,
I suggest that you make 12 shells so as to be sure of
getting 6 usable ones.

For the garnish, combine the sugar and 1 cup water
in a medium saucepan over high heat and bring to a boil.
Remove from the heat and add the verbena leaves. Steep
for 30 minutes. Using a slotted spoon, remove the leaves
and place them on paper towels. Air-dry for 10 to 12 hours,
turning them over while they are drying. Stored in an
airtight container, they will last for a week.

For the sauce, place the sugar in a saucepan and melt
over a high flame. Stir gently once the sugar begins to
color. As the caramel reaches a light gold, add ⅓ cup
water. Stir to dissolve the caramel. Add the betel leaves.
Reduce the heat and simmer for 1 minute. Switch off the
heat and steep for 5 minutes. Strain the sauce into a small
bowl, cover, and store in a cool place.

{CONTINUED}

{See page 192 for the Tart Shells recipe. As noted above, I'm recommending that you make the 12
shells yielded there, so that you will have at least 6 unbroken ones for these verbena-chocolate tarts.}

For the verbena-chocolate ganache, combine the cream and corn syrup in a heavy medium saucepan and bring to a boil over a medium flame. Add the verbena leaves, remove from the heat, and steep for 2 minutes. Bring to a boil again over a medium flame.

Place the chocolate in a heatproof bowl and slowly strain in the cream. Whisk continuously until the chocolate has melted. Whisk in the butter. Cool to room temperature. Whisk again. Cover the bowl with plastic and refrigerate for at least 1 hour.

Fill the tart shells with ganache, place the verbena leaves on top, and serve with a drizzle of the betel leaf sauce.

VERBENA leaves have a strong lemon scent that is often infused into perfumes, soaps, and potpourris. Their fragrance complements chocolate and pastries well, and the leaves also make an excellent addition to teas, broths, and cold drinks.

BETEL LEAVES, from the betel palm native to South Asia, contain a natural narcotic stimulant and have been chewed for several thousand years. Betel leaves, areca nut, and mineral lime combine to form the betel quid, which is chewed all over Asia, usually after meals, and induces mild euphoria. It turns the saliva bright red; in India, one sometimes sees entire streets splattered with bright red spots. The custom, though popular, may be hazardous: although chewing the betel quid is not addictive, it can produce oral cancers in longtime users. But if betel is consumed in moderation, the stimulating, peppery taste of this leaf can be an unusual and intriguing addition to meals.

Green Tomato and Sweet Onion Tartare with Mint Ice and Pomegranate Jus

This is one of my favorite desserts. I adore green tomatoes, and the sweetness of the onion blends well with their tart flavor.

The mint ice must be prepared a few hours in advance so that it can set. Combine the sugar and 1 cup water in a small saucepan and bring to a boil. Reduce the heat, add the mint leaves, and simmer for 3 minutes. Remove from the heat and cool in an ice bath.

Puree in a blender. Pour into a shallow metal container and freeze for 2 to 3 hours, until hard. Once it is solid, break it with an ice pick into approximately ⅓-inch pieces. Store in an airtight container in the freezer.

For the pomegranate jus, combine the juice, seeds, and sugar in a small saucepan. Simmer over a medium flame about 30 minutes, until it becomes thick (that is, until it is reduced by one-third). Strain the jus into a small bowl and cool to room temperature.

For the tartare, remove the stem ends and core from the tomatoes. Cut the tomatoes crosswise into thin slices. Gently toss in a large bowl with 1 tablespoon of the sugar. Cover and refrigerate for 1 hour.

4 SERVINGS

FOR THE MINT ICE
⅓ cup sugar
1 cup loosely packed mint leaves (any kind)

FOR THE POMEGRANATE JUS
2 cups pure pomegranate juice (such as Kalustyan's)
2 tablespoons dried pomegranate seeds (see Suppliers List, page 197)
¾ cup sugar

FOR THE TARTARE
3 medium green tomatoes
1½ cups plus 1 tablespoon sugar
1 Vidalia onion, thinly sliced lengthwise
4 bay leaves

{CONTINUED}

In the meanwhile, place ⅓ cup water, the remaining 1½ cups sugar, the onion, and the bay leaves in a medium saucepan. Cook over a medium-low flame, stirring from time to time, until the onions are soft and translucent and the liquid has evaporated, about 40 minutes. Remove from the heat and cool to room temperature. Remove the bay leaves.

Set a 4-inch pastry ring in the center of a serving plate and, within it, make a circular layer of four or five tomato slices. Set 1 teaspoon of onions on top of the tomatoes, and place another three to five alternating layers of tomato and onion. As you add each layer, press down on the stack to help stabilize it. Carefully remove the pastry ring. Set a small amount of onions on top. Repeat for the remaining 3 servings.

Drizzle pomegranate jus around the tartare and scatter a tablespoon of the ice on the plate. Serve immediately.

BAY LEAVES are used as a flavoring but not eaten whole. Just toss one or two of these pungent, slightly bitter leaves into simmering vegetables, broths, or sauces, and remove before serving. Because the leaves can be stored for several months, you can keep them around to enliven all kinds of dishes. Bay leaves come from the bay laurel tree and have long been a staple of Mediterranean cooking. The Greeks and Romans considered them so important that wreaths of bay leaves were set on the heads of champion athletes and star poets as a symbol of honor–hence the term *poet laureate*. Bay leaves have been used for a wide variety of medical applications throughout their history; now, one might chew on them to treat headaches or high blood sugar. Even for those in perfect health, bay leaves are an excellent stimulant.

ALOE plants, native to the eastern and southern regions of Africa, have long, spiky leaves that taper to a point. Beneath the thick exterior is a gentle, cool gel that can soothe irritated skin and relieve pain. Aloe gel is most popular for relief from sunburn, and is also said to clear acne and eliminate dandruff. Because of its moisturizing action, aloe makes the skin appear younger and more robust; it is believed, for example, that Cleopatra had aloe rubbed all over her body every day. Though the gel is somewhat uncommon in the kitchen, its dry, slightly bitter taste is an elegant and straightforward addition to sauces and soups.

Aloe-Chestnut Consommé

6 SERVINGS

1 pound fresh chestnuts
4 aloe vera leaves, 14-inch
   (see Suppliers List, page 197)
½ cup sugar
2 cinnamon sticks, each about 3
   inches long

This is a perfect palate cleanser, either before dessert or before a main course. The nuttiness of the base partners very well with the dry aloe flavor.

Preheat the oven to 375°F. Carefully score the flat side of the chestnuts with a paring knife. Set them on a baking sheet and roast for 25 minutes. Remove from the oven and when cool enough to handle, shell them, remove and discard the brown inner skin, and set aside.

Slice open the aloe leaves and scoop out the gel. In a medium (12-inch) saucepan, combine the gel, the sugar, cinnamon, chestnuts, and 3 cups water. Bring to a boil over a medium flame.

Reduce the heat and simmer for 20 minutes, or until the flavor of the chestnuts is detectable. Transfer to a bowl, cover, and refrigerate overnight.

Strain the consommé through cheesecloth, reserving a few chestnuts. Place one chestnut in each bowl and serve with ⅓ cup of cold consommé.

Sugared Shiso with Passionfruit Gelée

The beautiful shiso leaf is a marvel for the eyes, and offers an exotic flavor when mingled with the tartness of passionfruit.

FOR THE SUGARED SHISO
1 cup sugar
1 medium egg white
10 shiso leaves
    (see Suppliers List, page 197)

FOR THE GELÉE
3 gelatin sheets
    (see Suppliers List, page 197)
1 cup passionfruit puree
    (see Suppliers List, page 197)
½ cup superfine sugar

SHISO LEAVES, also known as perilla or beefsteak leaves, have a slightly bitter, minty taste that is popular in Asian cuisine, whether rolled into sushi or sprinkled over meat. The leaves are cultivated all over Asia in both green and red forms; green shiso has hints of cinnamon and ginger in addition to the mint-like base, and red shiso is excellent for imparting a purple color to savory dishes. Both have sharp, pointed tips all around; they are thought to boost immunity and promote digestion.

For the sugared shiso, line a baking sheet with parchment paper. Place the sugar in a shallow bowl.

Whisk together the egg white and 1 tablespoon water in a small bowl. Using your fingers, smear this very lightly on both sides of each shiso leaf.

Dredge the leaves in the sugar and place on the baking sheet. Air-dry the leaves for 6 hours, turning them over while they dry.

For the gelée, place the gelatin sheets in a bowl of cold water.

Combine the passionfruit and sugar in a blender. Place half the puree in a heatproof bowl and heat in the microwave until hot.

Remove the gelatin from the water and wring out the excess liquid, as if from a towel. Add the gelatin to the hot puree and whisk until completely dissolved. Whisk in the remaining puree.

Pour into a baking pan 6 inches square by 3 inches deep (or a similar size). Refrigerate for approximately 3 hours, until set.

Using a ring cutter, cut out pieces of gelée about ½ inch across. (You will get as many as 144 pieces. This is a petit four, and usage differs: a single serving might consist of 4 to 14 pieces.) Place them on the sugared shiso leaves and serve.

Basil Cocktail

FOR THE LYCHEE-LIME GELÉE
3 gelatin sheets
   (see Suppliers List, page 197)
10 fresh lychees, peeled and
   seeded
½ cup freshly squeezed lime juice
1 cup sugar

FOR THE BASIL SOUP
½ cup sugar
Leaves (stems removed) of
   2 medium bunches of
   basil (about 2 quarts, lightly
   packed); you can use Thai
   basil or any other variety

FOR THE BASIL SEEDS
1 tablespoon basil seeds
   (see Suppliers List, page 197)
3 tablespoons tequila (any kind)

This is a tantalizing, much-awaited drink after a long day in a sweltering kitchen. The basil cocktail consists of three separate layers—a lychee-lime gelée, a chilled soup, and bloomed basil seeds.

For the lychee-lime gelée, place the gelatin sheets in a bowl of cold water.

In a blender, puree the lychees with the lime juice and sugar. Place half the puree in a small bowl and heat in the microwave until hot.

Remove the gelatin from the water and wring out excess liquid, as if from a towel. Add the gelatin to the hot puree, and stir until completely dissolved. Stir in the rest of the lychee puree.

Pour into a 5-by-5-by-⅓-inch baking dish. Refrigerate until set. Cut it into ½-inch squares.

For the basil soup, prepare an ice bath.

Combine the sugar and 2 cups water in a medium saucepan and bring to a boil. Add the basil and cook for 2 minutes. Remove the basil with a slotted spoon and immediately place in the ice bath. When cold, transfer the leaves to paper towels to drain and set aside.

{CONTINUED}

BASIL, native to India and Persia, is a worldwide culinary staple from the mint family that appears in more than five hundred varieties. In Italian folklore, a woman places a pot of basil on her balcony to signal her lover; and in Romania, when a man accepts basil from a woman, the two are engaged. Hindu families regard basil as sacred and worship the plant in their homes, and in Africa it is still believed to protect one from scorpions. Basil has a strong, clove-like aroma mingled with a sweet bouquet and an ineffable flavor reminiscent of anise and mint. Throughout history, the scent of the leaf has been used to clear headaches and stuffiness. Some have even argued that basil can lower blood pressure and cholesterol.

Cool the pan of sugar water in the ice bath. Place in a blender with the basil leaves and blend until liquefied. Refrigerate until cold.

For the basil seeds, heat ½ cup water in a small bowl in the microwave until warm. Stir in the basil seeds. After 5 minutes, add the tequila. As the basil seeds sit in the liquid, they will absorb the moisture and bloom. As this occurs, their size will noticeably increase.

To prepare the cocktail, pour 1 inch of the basil seeds, with the liquid, into a Champagne flute, followed by a 1-inch layer of the gelée squares. Pour in the basil soup until the flute is almost full (you may have some soup left over), and add 1 more spoonful of basil seeds. The layers may shift as the drink is being constructed. As a garnish, place a square of gelée on a cocktail skewer, and set on top of the glass.

Apple-Rosemary Brioche

This brioche is a great morning pastry, a hearty snack during the winter, or an elegant warm dessert. Acacia honey has a smooth flavor that is floral and not exceedingly sweet.

For the pastry cream, place the milk in a medium saucepan and bring to a boil over a medium flame.

Sift the cornstarch and sugar into a small heatproof bowl and stir in the rosemary. Whisk in the yolk and egg. Slowly add about half of the hot milk while whisking continuously. Pour the mixture back into the saucepan with the hot milk.

Whisk continuously until it begins to bubble, reduce the heat to low, and cook for 1 minute while continuing to whisk vigorously.

Remove from the heat and pour into a clean bowl. Cover with plastic, pressing the plastic down into the bowl so it touches the surface. (This will prevent a skin from forming.) Set aside and cool to room temperature. Transfer to a piping bag with a no. 2 plain tip.

Preheat the oven to 350°F.

{CONTINUED}

{See page 188 for the Brioche Dough recipe.}

6 SERVINGS

FOR THE PASTRY CREAM
2 cups milk
⅓ cup cornstarch
⅓ cup sugar
Leaves from 2 sprigs of
  rosemary, chopped (about
  2 teaspoons)
1 medium egg yolk
1 medium whole egg

FOR THE APPLES
6 Fuji apples or any baking
  apples
½ cup acacia honey
  (see Suppliers List, page 197)
5 tablespoons unsalted butter,
  melted
2 sprigs of rosemary

FOR THE GLAZE
1 cup acacia honey
⅓ cup Cognac

Roll out the brioche dough until it is ⅕ inch thick. Cut into six 3-inch circles. Spray six 3-inch ring molds with oil. Place the circles of dough into the pans, spray with oil, and set in a warm area for 20 minutes.

For the apples, peel, core, and slice the apples ⅓ inch thick, and toss in a large bowl with the honey, melted butter, and rosemary. Spread the slices on a nonstick baking sheet and bake for 15 minutes, until they are almost cooked through. Discard the rosemary.

Pipe a dollop of the pastry cream onto the center of each disc of dough. Place the apple slices on top, fanning them around in a complete circle.

Bake 12 to 15 minutes, until the brioches are a light golden brown. Remove the brioches from the pans.

Whisk together the honey and Cognac, and brush all over the brioches.

ROSEMARY, native to the Mediterranean region, has been a symbol of memory and love for many centuries. Wedding guests would receive this sweet, pine-scented herb to signify that the bride and groom, though starting a new life, would not soon forget them. A sprig of rosemary placed under the pillow was believed to bring dreams of future loves. The needle-shaped leaves are often sold dried, but it is better to use fresh sprigs. Rosemary is thought to stimulate the circulatory and nervous systems, as well as promote the digestion of heavy and starchy foods.

Dill Ice Cream

The fragrance of dill surrounds you when you eat this ice cream. This is a recipe that I make with kids at Candy Camp, my cooking classes for children.

1 QUART

2 cups milk
2 cups heavy cream
½ cup sugar
2 stalks dill (the stems, without the leaves)
1 cup fresh dill leaves, loosely packed
12 medium egg yolks

Combine the milk, the cream, and ¼ cup of the sugar in a medium saucepan over a high flame. Once it reaches a boil, add the dill stalks. Switch off the heat and steep for 10 minutes.

Bring back to a boil. Stir in ½ cup of the dill leaves.

In a medium heatproof bowl, whisk together the egg yolks and remaining ¼ cup sugar. While whisking, slowly add half of the hot milk mixture. Pour this back into the saucepan with the hot milk. Whisk for 10 seconds. Remove from the heat.

Cool in an ice bath. Strain through a fine sieve. Add the remaining dill leaves. Puree the liquid in a blender. Process in an ice-cream machine according to the manufacturer's directions and transfer to the freezer.

DILL is believed to have calming qualities; the ancient Greeks would garland their heads with this herb to induce sleep. It has been used for more than three thousand years to cure hiccups and aid digestion. The whole plant is aromatic, and its long, feathery leaves can be used to accent the flavors of soups, sauces, or pastries. Once the plant begins to flower and mature, it produces slightly bitter seeds reminiscent of caraway, most famously used to flavor cucumber pickles.

Strawberry-Lemongrass Jam

2 PINTS

1 pound farmers' market
   strawberries, cleaned
4 cups sugar
Grated zest of 4 limes
1 cup strawberry puree
   (see Suppliers List, page 197);
   or make your own puree, as
   noted below, using 1 additional
   pound of strawberries
6 stalks lemongrass, tough outer
   leaves removed

Whenever I visit the farmers' market, I am drawn by the perfume of the strawberries and seduced into buying too many of them. In order to make sure nothing goes to waste, I take all the extras and make jam, which can be stored for a long time and has dozens of culinary applications. I like adding lemongrass, as it gives a nice lemon scent and goes well with strawberries.

NOTE: If the strawberry puree specified in the ingredients list is unavailable, you can make your own by mashing 1 additional pound of strawberries in a food processor and then reducing the puree to 1 cup in a saucepan over medium heat.

Toss the strawberries, sugar, zest, and strawberry puree in a large bowl. Cover and refrigerate for at least 10 hours.

Transfer to a large heavy saucepan, and place over a medium-low flame, stirring occasionally. Cook the jam until its volume is reduced by half, about 1 hour.

Using a slotted spoon, remove the whole strawberries and set them aside.

{CONTINUED}

With the back of a heavy knife, smash the stalks of lemongrass to break up the fibers. Cut the lemongrass into 2-inch lengths. Add the lemongrass to the jam and cook to 225°F, using a candy thermometer. Remove from the heat. Using a slotted spoon, carefully remove the lemongrass. Add back the whole strawberries and simmer for 15 minutes on low to medium heat.

Remove the jam from the heat and allow it cool. Ladle into two airtight 2-cup jars. Keep refrigerated.

LEMONGRASS is an aromatic tropical herb native to southern India and Ceylon. It is one of the main sources for lemon scents in commercial products, and the citrus flavor is a common addition to dishes in Caribbean and Asian cuisine. Lemongrass resembles pale, tender bamboo, with light green blade-like leaves with a dense woody base. The leaves and the stalk lend a pronounced lemon flavor. Lemongrass tea is also quite good and showcases the herb's power to induce sleep. It has antibacterial properties.

Chive Biscuits

18 BISCUITS

3½ cups bread flour
¼ cup sugar
1 teaspoon kosher salt
½ pound (2 sticks) unsalted
   butter, at room temperature
⅓ cup heavy cream
4 medium eggs
½ cup chopped fresh chives
1 tablespoon baking powder

The best part of baking biscuits is the smell that comes from the oven. Also, this is a great, quick alternative to making bread.

Preheat the oven to 325°F.

Combine the flour, sugar, salt, and butter in the bowl of a standing mixer with a paddle attachment and beat on medium-high speed until well blended, about 1 minute. Add the cream, eggs, chives, and baking powder. Mix for about 30 seconds more. (And that's all—don't overmix!)

On a floured surface, roll out the dough to a 6- by 3-inch rectangle about 1 inch thick, and with a sharp knife cut into 1-inch cubes.

Place the cubes on a nonstick baking sheet, and bake until light gold, about 7 minutes. Serve warm or at room temperature.

CHIVES are a member of the lily family; they have long, hollow leaves and a mild flavor like that of garlic and onion. Their first documented use was in China more than five thousand years ago, and it is thought that Marco Polo introduced them to Europe. Chives have high levels of vitamins A and C, and are said to stimulate the appetite and to promote digestion.

Mace Bhakras (Doughnuts)

This Persian doughnut is more bready than the American kind, but it has great texture, and the fragrance of mace invigorates the system.

15 DOUGHNUTS

1 tablespoon clarified butter
  (see Suppliers List, page 197)
½ cup sugar
3 medium eggs
1 cup semolina (ground
  semolina, which resembles
  Cream of Wheat or farina)
⅔ cup all-purpose flour
½ cup bread flour
1 tablespoon ground mace
¾ teaspoon baking powder
1 tablespoon unflavored yogurt
1 quart grapeseed oil, for frying

Beat the clarified butter and sugar in the bowl of a standing mixer with a paddle attachment on high speed for 3 minutes.

Reduce the mixer speed to low and add one egg at a time. With the beater still continuing to run on low, sift in the semolina and all-purpose flour. Sift together the bread flour, mace, and baking powder, and, with the beater still running on low, add to the dough.

Add the yogurt and return to high speed. Mix for another 20 seconds.

Remove the bowl and paddle from the mixer. Cover the dough with plastic and leave at room temperature for about 3 hours.

Heat the oil in a deep heavy pot to 320°F.

Tear off small pieces of the dough and roll into balls about ½ inch in diameter. (Dip your palms in additional semolina if the dough is too sticky to handle.)

Fry the dough a few pieces at a time until light brown, about 5 minutes. Remove with a slotted spoon and drain on paper towels.

Serve at room temperature.

{CONTINUED}

MACE is derived from the scarlet-colored fibrous outer cover of the nutmeg seed, which is native to the islands of eastern Indonesia. When dried, mace turns yellow or orange and is sold whole or ground. A piece of unground mace is known as a "blade." Mace has an aroma similar to but subtler than that of nutmeg; because the yield of mace per fruit is far less, mace is more expensive. Mace is an excellent choice when one wishes to add the flavor of nutmeg to a light-colored dish but does not want dark specks in the final product. It is believed that mace can promote digestion.

Steamed Chocolate Buns
with Cinnamon Crème Fraîche

12 BUNS

FOR THE CRÈME FRAÎCHE
2 cups buttermilk
1 cup heavy cream
4 cinnamon sticks, each about
   3 inches long

FOR THE BUNS
⅓ cup granulated sugar
2 tablespoons finely ground
   coffee
12 frozen plain steamed buns,
   thawed (see Suppliers List,
   page 197)
1¼ cups finely chopped dark
   chocolate (about 12 ounces)
1¼ cups finely chopped milk
   chocolate (about 12 ounces)
½ cup raw sugar

This is one of the most popular desserts at my restaurant, Graffiti. The spongy texture of the bun is an excellent counterpoint to the melted chocolate and crisp caramelized sugar.

The crème fraîche needs to be prepared a day in advance. Combine the buttermilk, heavy cream, and cinnamon in a medium bowl and whisk for 30 seconds. Keeping the cinnamon in the mixture, place a wet towel over the bowl and leave at room temperature for 24 hours. Store in the refrigerator (still keeping the cinnamon in the mixture).

For the chocolate buns, mix together the granulated sugar and the coffee. Sprinkle two pinches into each bun, and add 1 tablespoon of each chocolate per bun. (Note: These buns always come closed on one side but open on the other, somewhat like an envelope, so that they can be stuffed.)

Place the buns in a steamer, cover, and steam for 3 minutes.

Remove the buns and sprinkle them with raw sugar. Caramelize the sugar with a blowtorch. Serve warm with the crème fraîche.

{CONTINUED}

NOTE: To set up a steamer, bring a few inches of water to a boil in a wok, large pot, or deep skillet. Place a perforated pan, steamer basket, or metal rack on top, not touching the water. You could also use a rice cooker with a steaming attachment.

CINNAMON was prized as a mysterious spice in early European civilization; at one point it was worth more than fifteen times its weight in silver. The Arab traders who brought cinnamon to the West kept their sources a closely guarded secret and made up elaborate stories about how the spice was acquired. According to one story, birds built nests out of cinnamon sticks high atop cliffs; in order to obtain the spice, it was necessary to trick the birds into placing heavy pieces of meat in their nests, and then collect the cinnamon sticks when the nests fell. People were naturally skeptical about such stories, and the search for cinnamon became an impetus for world expansion. When the Portuguese finally discovered cinnamon trees on the island of Ceylon, now Sri Lanka, the possession of cinnamon became the object of an international struggle. Cinnamon, as everyone now knows, is the inner bark of the cinnamon tree. The bark of the cassia tree has a slightly bitter aroma and is known as Chinese cinnamon, but Ceylon cinnamon is much sweeter and milder. In ayurveda, it is believed that cinnamon is a detoxifying agent, which strengthens and energizes tissues.

Naan Kahtai (Cardamom Cookies)

This is a traditional cookie consumed by Gujaratis in India. It is a great eggless cookie, packed with cardamom flavor, and has a sandy, crunchy texture.

60 COOKIES

½ teaspoon ground cloves
1½ teaspoons crushed
  cardamom seeds
½ teaspoon freshly grated
  nutmeg
4 cups all-purpose flour
4 cups farina
1 pound clarified butter
  (see Suppliers List, page 197),
  as weighed after the milk
  solids have been removed
4 cups sugar
1 vanilla bean

Combine the cloves, cardamom, and nutmeg.

Sift together the flour and farina.

Place the butter and sugar in the bowl of a standing mixer and beat on high speed with a paddle attachment for 5 minutes, or until the butter is light and fluffy.

Reduce the speed to medium and add the sifted flour and the spices. Split the vanilla bean lengthwise and scrape in the contents. (Note: You can make vanilla sugar for later use by storing the bean pods in sugar.) Continue to mix until a dough forms, about 2 minutes. Transfer the dough to a bowl and cover. Leave at room temperature for about 6 hours.

Preheat the oven to 300°F. Line 2 baking sheets with parchment paper and spray them with oil.

Knead the dough slightly. Tear off pieces of dough and roll into balls about 1 inch in diameter. Set the balls on the baking sheets. With the palm of your hand, flatten them slightly.

Bake the cookies for about 40 minutes, or until lightly golden. Cool, then store them in an airtight box.

{CONTINUED}

CLOVES have a strong, pungent, sweet aroma. These unopened flower buds are pink when picked and turn brown when dried. Their intense, fiery taste is instantly recognizable in any dessert or sauce; in Indonesia, cigarettes often contain cloves, and thus their smell hangs in the air of most public spaces. Cloves have been used in Asia for thousands of years, and it is believed that members of the ancient Chinese court would chew on them to freshen their breath before addressing the emperor. Ayurvedics believe that clove prevents toothaches or lessens the pain of a toothache which has already begun.

CARDAMOM is the seed of a tropical fruit in the ginger family and is native to southern India. The seeds are found inside oval-shaped fruit pods. When the pods ripen they must be picked by hand; for this reason, cardamom is one of the most expensive spices available, but its delicate, fragrant aroma and astringent taste, punctuated by notes of camphor and eucalyptus, are certainly worth the cost. Cardamom is not especially popular in Europe, with the notable exception of Scandinavia: the Vikings, upon trying cardamom in Constantinople, loved the spice so much they brought it home, where it has since become a common ingredient in pastries. The Greeks and Romans imported it as a digestive aid.

NUTMEG, native to eastern Indonesia, is the inner brown seed of the same fruit that provides mace. It has an instantly recognizable punch that has made its scent a common addition to incenses and soaps. In India, the spice is used nearly exclusively in desserts, although European cuisine has adopted it for savory applications as well. In any case, it should be used with care: nutmeg contains a chemical called myristicin that reportedly has hallucinogenic effects, and eating too much nutmeg can actually be fatal. Ironically, nutmeg was used in the hope of staving off death during the Middle Ages, when it was thought to protect households from the plague. Nutmeg powder prevents bad breath and heals indigestion. In the Middle East, nutmeg is considered an aphrodisiac.

Mango-Mâche-Asafetida Salad with Lime Sherbet

6 SERVINGS

FOR THE LIME SHERBET
3 cups milk
½ cup sugar
1 cup freshly squeezed lime juice

FOR THE DRESSING
½ cup mango puree
    (see Suppliers List, page 197)
½ teaspoon asafetida
    (see Suppliers List, page 197)
Pinch of kosher salt
1 teaspoon sugar
⅓ cup pistachio oil
    (see Suppliers List, page 197)

FOR THE SALAD
2 mangoes, peeled
12 ounces mâche or (if mâche is
    unavailable) red-leaf lettuce,
    cut into small pieces
½ cup shelled unsalted pistachios
1 cup crystallized ginger

{See page 90 for the Crystallized Ginger recipe.}

This light dessert has a subtle savory twist that is extremely refreshing.

For the lime sherbet, whisk together the milk and sugar in a small saucepan and heat over a medium flame until the sugar is dissolved. Remove from the heat and cool in an ice bath. Stir in the lime juice. Process in an ice-cream machine according to the manufacturer's instructions, then put in the freezer until needed.

For the dressing, combine the mango puree, asafetida, salt, and sugar in a large bowl and whisk together. Slowly drizzle in the oil, continuing to whisk, until an emulsion is created.

For the salad, either cut the mangoes into thin slices with a knife or mandoline, or peel off thin slices with a peeler.

Add the mango slices, mâche, and pistachios to the dressing. Cut the crystallized ginger into fine julienne, add to the salad, and toss to combine. (The recipe for Crystallized Ginger makes 1 cup, all of which should be used here.) Arrange in a small mound on each plate. On top, set a scoop of the lime sherbet.

{CONTINUED}

ASAFETIDA is called "devil's crap" in many languages, and a deep whiff of the spice will quickly explain this unflattering epithet. Nonetheless, it is used extensively in vegetarian dishes in India, and explicit references to it appear in ancient Indian texts. The name "asafetida" is derived from two languages: *assa* is a Latinized form of the Farsi for "resin mastic," and the Latin *foetidus* means "smelling fetid." This spice contains a wealth of sulfur compounds. It is sold either as a gum or, more commonly, ground into powder.

SEELS

NUTS

GRAINS

LEGUMES

Poppyseed Cake

The rare, intense flavor of poppyseeds penetrates the entire cake.

Place the butter and sugar in the bowl of a standing mixer, and beat on high speed with a paddle attachment until the butter is fluffy and light, about 5 minutes. Add the corn syrup, and beat for another 5 minutes.

Sift together the flour and baking powder. Reduce the mixer speed to medium and add the flour mixture, the poppyseeds, and salt.

After the dry ingredients are incorporated, add one egg yolk at a time, making sure each is completely incorporated before adding the next. Add the milk and mix for 1 minute more.

Transfer the batter to a medium bowl, cover with plastic, and refrigerate for 2 hours.

Preheat the oven to 325°F. Spray two 9-inch pie plates with oil.

Pour in the batter until each is three-quarters full. Sprinkle additional poppyseeds over the top. Bake for 15 to 20 minutes, until a toothpick placed in the center of the cake comes out dry. Store in an airtight box.

❂ TWO 9-INCH CAKES,
OR 8 SERVINGS

8 tablespoons (1 stick)
  unsalted butter
⅓ cup sugar
¼ cup light corn syrup
1 cup all-purpose flour
2 teaspoons baking powder
2 tablespoons poppyseeds,
  plus extra for baking
Pinch of kosher salt
6 medium egg yolks
⅓ cup milk

{CONTINUED}

POPPYSEEDS are from the famous opium-producing poppy plant native to India, Iran, and the eastern Mediterranean region. Fortunately (or unfortunately) the psychoactive chemicals in the poppyseed evaporate during ripening; nonetheless, poppyseeds are an excellent remedy for insomnia, and are also rich in vitamin C. The seeds have a pleasant, nutty taste that goes well in many baked goods.

Sweet Rice with Mango and Sunflower Seeds

6 SERVINGS

1 cup jasmine rice

2 cups hot water

½ teaspoon mango powder
   (sold as amchoor; see Suppliers
   List, page 197)

2 tablespoons sugar

Pinch of kosher salt

¾ cup unsalted hulled sunflower
   seeds

2 cups medium-diced mango
   (about 2 medium mangoes)

The thick rice softens the intense flavors of the mango and sunflower seeds in this rich, satisfying dessert.

Heat the oven to 350°F.

Place the rice, water, mango powder, sugar, and salt in a medium saucepan. Stir and bring to a full boil over a high flame.

Reduce the heat to low, cover, and simmer for about 16 minutes, or until cooked. Spread the rice on a baking sheet to cool.

In the meanwhile, place the sunflower seeds on another baking sheet, and place in the oven for 4 to 5 minutes until toasted. Remove from the oven and allow to cool down a bit.

Add the mango and sunflower seeds to the rice and mix everything together. Serve slightly warm.

SUNFLOWER SEEDS, though usually just salted and eaten as a snack, can also be used to add a suggestive nutty taste to salads, as a garnish. They were first cultivated by the Ozark Bluff dwellers in the western plains of North America several thousand years ago. The seeds figured prominently in many Native American diets and were even placed next to the graves of hunters as sustenance for their journey into the afterlife. Today, sunflower seeds remain one of the best sources of vitamin E.

FENUGREEK is popular in the Mediterranean and plays a major part in the average diet in countries like Yemen. The spice is derived from fenugreek seeds, which have a sweet taste that is sometimes used to make imitation maple syrup. (In fact, the consumption of fenugreek can make one's sweat smell like maple syrup!) The grooved, oblong seeds are yellowish brown. Fenugreek's species name means "Greek hay," in reference to the once common practice of adding fenugreek to hay in order to liven it up and increase its appeal to grazing cows. Though its medical value for humans is not proved, recent evidence suggests that fenugreek may help fight diabetes. Fenugreek water is thought to be an effective laxative.

Fenugreek Financier

12 SERVINGS

¼ cup fenugreek seeds
   (see Suppliers List, page 197)
⅓ cup honey, such as acacia
   honey
1 pound (4 sticks) unsalted butter
3 cups confectioners' sugar
1½ cups all-purpose flour
2 cups almond flour
   (see Suppliers List, page 197)
2 cups (14 to 16 large) egg whites

The bitterness of fenugreek combines well with the nuttiness of the brown butter in this aromatic cake.

Soak the fenugreek seeds overnight in 2 cups water to soften them.

Drain the seeds. (Fenugreek water is believed to be very healthy to drink, so you should at least have a taste before discarding it.) Use a mallet to flatten the seeds; then mix them with the honey in a small bowl.

Melt the butter in a medium saucepan over a medium flame. Heat until it has a nutty aroma and turns light brown. Pour the butter into the honey and fenugreek while whisking.

Sift the confectioners' sugar, flour, and almond flour together into a large bowl. Add the butter mixture and whisk together until smooth. Add the egg whites and continue to whisk vigorously until smooth. Cover and refrigerate for 2 hours.

Preheat the oven to 350°F.

Spray twelve 4 x 2 x ¾-inch rectangular molds with oil.

Pour in the batter until the molds are ¾ full (you could try other size molds as well).

Bake for 12 minutes or until golden brown. Cool, then store in an airtight box.

Falooda with Fresh Strawberry Ice Cream

This is a traditional and refreshing summertime drink that one might purchase on the pavements of Bombay, though it originated in Persia.

4 SERVINGS

FOR THE BASE
1 quart milk
2½ cups diced strawberries
   (1½ pints whole berries)

FOR THE BASIL SEEDS
3 tablespoons sugar
5 sprigs of fresh mint
¼ cup basil seeds
   (see Suppliers List, page 197)

FOR THE VERMICELLI
2 tablespoons sugar
2 tablespoons rose water
9 ounces vermicelli

1 cup diced fresh peeled and
   seeded lychees (1 pound)

See page 191 for the Strawberry Ice Cream recipe. You will need about half the amount yielded there.

For the base, place the milk and strawberries in a blender and puree until smooth. Chill in the refrigerator.

For the basil seeds, bring the sugar, mint, and 1 cup water to a boil in a small saucepan. Remove from the heat. Steep for 1 minute. Strain the liquid into a large bowl. Add the basil seeds (which will expand from the heat of the water). After 5 minutes, strain the basil seeds over a sink and set them aside.

For the vermicelli, combine the sugar, rose water, and 2 cups water in a medium saucepan and bring to a boil over a high flame. Add the vermicelli and cook until the noodles are al dente, about 5 minutes. Drain in a colander and cool.

To make the falooda, spoon some lychees into the bottom of four sundae glasses. Add the vermicelli, 1 tablespoon of the basil seeds, and some of the base. Add another layer each of the lychees, vermicelli, and base. Place some basil seeds and additional base on top, and finish with a scoop of the strawberry ice cream.

Cumin Seed Gougères with Sweet Mustard

FOR THE SWEET MUSTARD
⅓ cup Dijon or yellow mustard
½ cup heavy cream
⅓ cup sugar
1 medium egg yolk

FOR THE GOUGÈRES
1 cup milk
6 tablespoons (¾ stick) salted
   butter
1 cup all-purpose flour, sifted
5 medium whole eggs
½ cup grated Gruyère cheese
1 tablespoon crushed cumin
   seeds

These gougères are among the most addictive desserts I've ever experienced. The cumin gives them an unusual and unforgettable aroma.

For the mustard sauce, combine the mustard, heavy cream, sugar, and egg yolk in a medium saucepan. Whisk continuously over a very low flame until the sugar dissolves and the mixture thickens, about 5 minutes. Set aside at room temperature.

Preheat the oven to 410°F. Line two baking sheets with parchment paper.

In a medium saucepan, bring the milk and butter to a boil over a high flame. Stir occasionally with a wooden spoon to avoid scorching.

Add the flour, reduce the heat to low, and stir vigorously with the wooden spoon. Keep stirring until the dough no longer sticks to the sides of the pan and becomes a mound in the center of the pan.

Transfer the dough to the bowl of a standing mixer with a paddle attachment. Mix at low speed and add one egg at a time, making sure each is completely incorporated before adding the next.

{CONTINUED}

Reserve 2 tablespoons of the Gruyère and ¾ teaspoon of the cumin seeds, and blend the remainder into the dough with the mixer still on.

Transfer the dough to a piping bag with a no. 5 round tip, and squeeze out about 108 teaspoon-size balls onto the baking sheets. Leave approximately 2 inches of space between the balls, since they will expand during baking.

Sprinkle the reserved Gruyère and cumin seeds over the balls and bake for 15 to 18 minutes, until golden brown.

Place each gougère on a small dollop of the sweet mustard sauce and serve warm, 6 gougères to a serving.

CUMIN seeds have a strong, warm, bitter flavor that betrays their presence in any dish. A member of the parsley family, cumin is sold both as whole seeds and as a powder, with the best coming from Sri Lanka. The powder can lose its flavor easily, so it is better to keep the pale green seeds and crush them when needed. Though cumin is now primarily characteristic of Indian and Mexican cuisine, it was once widely used throughout the major ancient civilizations and probably originated in the Mediterranean region. In some places, it was such a staple that it was kept at the table in lieu of pepper, a practice still observed in Morocco. Cumin has long been known to promote digestion, and it is also a potent source of iron.

Fragrant Fennel Brittle

⅓ CUP OF BRITTLE PIECES

3 tablespoons fennel seeds
½ cup sugar

In India, fennel is almost always served at the end of a meal to freshen breath and promote digestion. Serve these crisps as a flavorful end to a large meal.

In a dry skillet, toast the fennel seeds over a high flame, stirring occasionally, until lightly toasted (about 2 minutes).

Place the sugar in a small saucepan and cook over a medium flame until light gold. Stir in the fennel seeds and let the caramel and seeds intermingle.

Remove from the heat and pour onto a nonstick baking mat. Place another mat on top. Press the top mat with a rolling pin to flatten and spread the mixture. Then remove the top mat and cool the mixture until it is brittle.

Break the brittle into small, bite-size pieces. Store in an airtight container.

NOTE: This is eaten like small breath mints, so the amount would be good for a week.

FENNEL SEEDS are oval light green seeds whose sweet taste is mingled with a flavor like licorice or anise. They can freshen the breath when chewed and are also appetite suppressants—a fact well known to the Puritans, who would chew them during fasting periods and church services. Seeds from Lucknow fennel of India are brighter, smaller, sweeter, and more aromatic than common fennel seeds; keep your eyes open for them in specialty markets.

Orange–Marcona Almond Salad with Pineapple Granita

A great dessert for summer. Not only is it light and refreshing, but it is also dairy- and gluten-free.

4 SERVINGS

⅓ cup sugar
2 cups pineapple juice
8 small navel oranges, peeled, segmented, seeded, and chilled (or any other variety of orange, such as a blood orange)
1 cup unsalted Marcona almonds (see Suppliers List, page 197)
1 tablespoon almond oil (see Suppliers List, page 197)
½ cup microherbs

For the pineapple granita, heat the sugar and 1 cup of the pineapple juice in a small saucepan until the sugar dissolves, stirring occasionally. Remove from the heat. Stir in the rest of the juice, and cool in an ice bath. Pour into a flat metal container such as a sheet tray, cover, and freeze. Once it becomes solid, break it with a fork so that it becomes flaky. Re-cover and return to the freezer.

For the salad, in a large bowl, toss together the oranges with the almonds, almond oil, and microherbs.

Serve on chilled plates with granita scattered around.

ALMONDS probably originated in western Asia, but their cultural significance is international. In traditional ayurvedic medicine, almonds are thought to strengthen memory. In Roman times, almonds were showered over newly married couples as a fertility blessing. Because the trees bloom so early in the year, their name in Hebrew is *shakad*, or "hasty awakening." Almonds may have derived their historical import at least in part from their nutritional value: they are higher in vitamin E than any other nut, and their high level of protein figures critically in some vegetarian diets. There are many varieties of almond trees, classified as either sweet or bitter, but only nuts from sweet almond trees are sold for consumption.

Pistachio Crème Brûlée

8 SERVINGS

2 cups heavy cream
1 cup milk
⅓ cup granulated sugar
1 cup pistachio paste
   (see Suppliers List, page 197)
9 medium egg yolks
½ cup raw sugar
Whole shelled unsalted
   pistachios, optional

Unlike most crèmes brûlées, this one is served out of the ramekin and rolled into small balls. This technique maximizes the crunchiness and is always a crowd-pleaser.

Preheat the oven to 350°F.

Combine the cream, milk, and about 2½ tablespoons of the sugar in a medium saucepan and bring to a boil over a high flame. Whisk in the pistachio paste. Remove from the heat.

In a medium heatproof bowl, whisk together the egg yolks and the remaining sugar. While whisking continuously, add half of the hot milk mixture. Return the combined mixture to the saucepan with the hot milk, and whisk to combine.

Strain into a 12-by-12-by-2-inch glass baking dish. Place the baking dish in a larger pan and pour hot water around it. (The water level should reach about half the height of the glass dish.) Cover with foil and bake 20 minutes, or until the custard sets.

{CONTINUED}

Remove the custard from the oven and set aside to cool. Cover the baking dish with plastic and freeze for 2 hours, or until firm.

Spread the raw sugar on a flat dish. Scoop out balls of custard with a small melon baller. Roll the balls in the raw sugar, to cover the entire surface of each ball, and set on a baking sheet. Using a blowtorch, caramelize the sugar.

Serve on a plate with whole pistachios, if desired.

PISTACHIOS are native to Asia Minor, where they were first eaten nearly nine thousand years ago. The Hanging Gardens of Babylon, one of the seven wonders of the ancient world, were said to contain pistachio trees, and pistachios are mentioned in the Old Testament, along with almonds. The Chinese believe the open shell of a pistachio looks like a smile, and so they call the pistachio the "happy nut." A Middle Eastern tale describes two lovers sitting under pistachio trees and listening to the shells burst open. When they were first commercialized, pistachios were sometimes dyed red to hide imperfections in the shell and stains from the picking process. Though now most pistachios are left in their natural beige, some red pistachios are still sold. Pistachios are rich in fiber, calcium, thiamin, iron, and vitamin A.

Hazelnut Crêpes with Caramel–Pine Nut Sauce

6 SERVINGS

FOR THE CRÊPES
⅓ cup milk
⅓ cup all-purpose flour
1 medium egg
1 tablespoon grapeseed oil
Pinch of freshly ground black
   pepper
Pinch of kosher salt
Pinch of sugar
Pinch of ground cinnamon

FOR THE HAZELNUT MOUSSE
2 vanilla beans
2 cups hazelnut paste
   (see Suppliers List, page 197)
2 cups heavy cream

FOR THE CARAMEL–PINE NUT
SAUCE
1 cup sugar
¾ cup heavy cream
¾ cup lightly toasted pine nuts

*This is one of my absolute favorite dishes at brunch.
I am always drawn to the crêpes for their great texture.*

For the crêpe batter, vigorously whisk together the milk, flour, egg, oil, pepper, salt, sugar, and cinnamon in a large bowl. Cover with plastic and refrigerate for about 1 hour.

In the meanwhile, for the hazelnut mousse, split the vanilla beans lengthwise and scrape the contents into a food processor. (Note: You can put the empty pods in a jar with sugar to make vanilla sugar for future use.) Add the hazelnut paste and cream, and process into a smooth paste. Transfer to a piping bag with a no. 2 plain tip and refrigerate.

For the caramel–pine nut sauce, place the sugar in a small saucepan and melt it over a medium flame. Only stir the sugar once it begins to color. When it is completely light gold, stir in the cream and nuts. (Be careful, as the cream will bubble up and may burn your hand.) Stir until the caramel has dissolved into the cream. Set aside.

{CONTINUED}

HAZELNUTS were considered by the ancient Chinese to be one of the five sacred foods given to man by the gods. Most probably, these nuts originated in northern Turkey around the Black Sea coastline. The Greek physician Dioscorides prescribed them for baldness, and the Roman chef Apicius included a recipe for hazelnut candy in his famous cookbook. Hazelnuts are also called filberts, a possible reference to St. Philibert's Day, which falls in mid-August, at about the time the earliest hazelnuts begin to ripen. Hazelnuts are rich in fiber, antioxidants, and vitamins C and E.

PINE NUTS, sometimes called Indian nuts, pignoli, or piñones, are the seeds of the pine tree. These nuts are expensive because they are so difficult to remove from the pinecones. They were an important food source for Native Americans, who consumed them thousands of years ago. They have long been cultivated in the Mediterranean as well. Pine nuts contain more protein than any other nut or seed. Pine nuts are difficult to keep fresh because of their high fat content and will quickly turn rancid if not stored in the refrigerator; the Romans used to preserve their pine nuts in honey. The Mediterranean variety, cultivated from the stone pine tree, is by far the most popular. Some markets also carry a more strongly flavored Chinese pine nut.

To make the crêpes, line a baking sheet with parchment paper. Heat a 6-inch nonstick crêpe or sauté pan over a medium flame and spray lightly with oil. Pour a thin layer of chilled batter into the hot pan, swirling around the pan until the batter reaches an even thickness. Cook the crêpe for 30 seconds per side. Place in one layer on the baking sheet. Repeat, using all the crêpe batter. Keep the cooked crêpes warm in the oven while cooking the rest.

Pipe hazelnut mousse onto the center of each crepe, roll up, and drizzle the caramel–pine nut sauce on them and around them on the plate.

Chocolate-Chile Tarts and Chocolate-Walnut Cakes

The spiciness of the chiles softens the strong, rich taste of chocolate in the tarts, and the nuttiness of the cake is exquisite.

 12 SERVINGS

FOR THE CHOCOLATE-WALNUT CAKES

⅓ cup sugar
8 tablespoons (1 stick) unsalted butter
2 medium eggs
1 teaspoon baking soda
1 cup cake flour, sifted
½ cup walnuts, toasted and roughly chopped
½ cup chopped dark chocolate (about 4½ ounces)

FOR THE CHOCOLATE-CHILE TARTS

1 dried red chile (with seeds), about 1½ inches long, chopped
3 cups heavy cream
2 tablespoons light corn syrup
1 cup chopped dark chocolate (about 9 ounces)
1 teaspoon walnut oil (see Suppliers List, page 197)
⅓ cup finely chopped walnuts
¼ cup cocoa powder
12 sheets brik dough (see Suppliers List, page 197) or phyllo

FOR THE SAUCE

⅓ cup grapeseed oil
3 dried red chiles (with seeds), each chile about 1½ inches long, chopped

{CONTINUED}

For the chocolate-walnut cakes, preheat the oven to 350°F and line a baking sheet with parchment paper.

Place the sugar and butter in the bowl of a standing mixer, and beat on high speed with a paddle attachment until the butter is fluffy and light, about 5 minutes.

Add the eggs, baking soda, flour, walnuts, and chocolate and mix at medium speed until incorporated. Remove the bowl and paddle from the mixer.

Tear off small pieces of the dough and roll into balls about 1½ inches across. Set them on the baking sheet and flatten them slightly with the palm of your hand.

Bake for 4 minutes; they should still be a little raw when they come out. Remove from the oven and cool. Trim off the edges of each cake with a 1½-inch ring cutter. Set aside to cool at room temperature.

For the chocolate-chile tarts, combine the chile and 2 cups of the cream in a medium saucepan over a medium flame. As the cream heats, whisk in the corn syrup. Bring to a boil, switch off the heat, and steep for 10 minutes.

Place the chocolate and walnut oil in a medium heat-proof bowl. Bring the cream back to a boil. Slowly strain through a fine sieve into the chocolate. Whisk until the chocolate is melted and smooth. Cover the ganache with plastic and refrigerate for at least 2 hours.

WALNUTS were so popular among the Romans and so well-liked that they were considered a royal food of the god Jove. They are believed to have originated in Persia, and received their current name when they were introduced to England (in Old English, *walhnutu* means "foreign nut"). Today most of the world's walnuts are produced in California. Walnuts are best purchased still in the shell. They are considered a good source of omega-3 fatty acids, which may lower one's risk of cardio-vascular disease.

Whisk the remaining cup of cream into the ganache. Fold in the chopped walnuts. Transfer the ganache to a piping bag fitted with a no. 2 plain tip, and set aside in the refrigerator.

Preheat the oven to 275°F. Spray twelve 3-inch ring molds with oil.

Combine the cocoa powder and ⅓ cup water in a small saucepan over a medium flame and heat until the mixture is smooth, stirring occasionally. Set aside to cool.

Cut at least three 4-inch circles from each of the brik dough sheets, and brush these on both sides with the cocoa water.

Stack 3 dough rounds one on top of the other in every ring mold, pressing them in to form a tart shell. Set a clean ovenproof paperweight inside, so that the shells stay flat when baking.

Bake the tart shells for about 6 minutes, or until crisp. Cool the shells briefly. Fill them with the ganache.

For the sauce, warm the oil in a small saucepan over a medium flame. When the oil is hot, add the crushed chiles and switch off the heat. Cool to room temperature. Strain the oil through a fine sieve and reserve.

To serve, drizzle some sauce on each dessert plate and arrange one tart and one cake on each plate.

Barley Legal

This drink is dedicated to all the young celebrities out there.

Soak the barley in 1 cup water for 5 hours. Strain and chill the liquid. Reserve the barley.

Muddle together the ginger, sugar, and orange juice in a cocktail shaker. Add a scoop of ice cubes, the barley water, and the Scotch. Shake together well.

Spoon 1 tablespoon of the barley into each of two Champagne flutes and add some ice cubes. (Discard any leftover barley.) Strain the liquid into the flutes, filling almost to the top, and garnish each glass with a cherry.

2 SERVINGS

½ cup pearl barley (or any kind available at the market)
1 small piece ginger (2-inch lobe)
1 tablespoon sugar
Juice of ½ orange
2 jiggers Johnny Walker Scotch
2 cherries

BARLEY has a history of promoting strength. Greek and Roman athletes believed it could improve performance; the Roman word for gladiator, *hordearii,* translates to "eater of barley." Barley water is also an ancient medical remedy thought to be energizing and nutritious, so much so that it has been sold at Wimbledon for more than seventy years. Under American law, products containing barley can advertise the grain's power to reduce the risk of coronary heart disease.

Rawa (Semolina Pudding)

4 SERVINGS

2 tablespoons clarified butter
   (see Suppliers List, page 197)
1 cup fine semolina
2½ cups milk
½ cup sugar
½ cup raisins
½ cup slivered almonds, toasted
⅓ cup charoli nuts, toasted
   (see Suppliers List, page 197)

This is a Persian delicacy that one always makes the first thing in the morning on auspicious days, for good luck. My aunts Khorshed and Zarine are the ones who prepare this great dessert brilliantly.

In a medium saucepan, heat the clarified butter over a low flame. Add the semolina and lightly sauté for 10 minutes.

Add the milk and sugar and simmer over a medium flame until the semolina is cooked through, about 10 minutes. If the semolina absorbs all the liquid before it is cooked, add more milk as needed.

Stir in the raisins, almonds, and charoli nuts, remove from the heat, and serve warm.

SEMOLINA is known as rawa in southern India. It is the endosperm or heart of the durum wheat kernel, a hard wheat variety, and is the most nutritional part of the kernel. It has a high protein-to-carbohydrate ratio and a very high gluten content, and is packed with fiber and minerals. Wheat germ, the heart of the wheat kernel, is believed to reduce cholesterol.

Granola

This simple blend of crunchy granola and smooth yogurt offers a perfect example of textural balance.

Preheat the oven to 250°F.

Combine the pistachios, cashews, oats, grapefruit juice, honey, lemon zest, raisins, and apricots in a large bowl.

Spread on a nonstick baking sheet and bake until the granola feels dry to the touch, about 1 hour. While it bakes, stir it every 5 minutes with a spatula.

Allow the granola to cool. Serve with yogurt and, if desired, a spoonful of acacia honey. Store in an airtight container.

1 cup unsalted pistachios, roughly chopped
1 cup raw cashews, roughly chopped
6 cups instant oats
½ cup freshly squeezed grapefruit juice
2 cups acacia honey, plus optional extra for serving (see Suppliers List, page 197)
Grated zest of 1 lemon
1 cup raisins
1 cup dried apricots, sliced
3 cups sheep's milk yogurt

OATS have been cultivated for thousands of years, though of all the grains they were by far the slowest to be adopted as food; they were seen primarily as weeds that only animals could enjoy— in the eighteenth century, Samuel Johnson joked that they were given only to horses in England, but to men in Scotland. Today, of course, oats are found in a wide range of foods, including cereals, granola, cookies, and breads. They are very high in soluble fiber that can help lower cholesterol, a finding that contributed to a brief oat bran craze in the 1980s, which inspired products like oat bran doughnuts and oat bran potato chips. Though the frenzy has passed, oats still remain one of the most nutritious foods one can consume.

Frangipane-Chickpea Cakes

This cake complements savory dishes such as braised lamb.

Preheat the oven to 350°F and spray nine 4-ounce cake pans with oil.

Combine the almond paste, sugar, and butter in the bowl of a standing mixer with a paddle attachment, and beat on high speed about 7 minutes, until completely mixed.

Reduce the speed to low and add one egg one at a time, making sure each is completely incorporated before adding the next. Add the chickpea flour and mix the dough for another 20 seconds.

Put the dough into the pans until each pan is three-quarters full. (If any dough is left over, store it in plastic wrap for later use; it should be used within 5 days.) Bake for 12 minutes, or until golden brown.

8 ounces almond paste
(see Suppliers List, page 197;
note: do *not* use marzipan)
2 cups sugar
½ pound (2 sticks) unsalted
butter
9 medium eggs
2 cups chickpea flour, sifted
(see Suppliers List, page 197)

CHICKPEAS, also known as garbanzo beans, are packed with protein and are well known to the world as the major ingredient of hummus–in fact, *hummus* means "chickpea" in Turkish. Chickpeas are available both dried and canned. Though dried chickpeas are always better, they require a lot of time to soak and cook. Most chickpeas found in the market are round and beige (the Kabuli type), but there are also red, green, brown, and black variants (the Desi type). Chickpeas are an excellent source of carbohydrates.

Dar Ni Puri (Lentil Cake)

FOR THE DAL

4 cups yellow lentils
   (see Suppliers List, page 197)
3 vanilla beans
4 cups sugar
½ cup slivered almonds
½ cup chopped unsalted pistachios
⅓ cup dried cherries
1 teaspoon freshly grated nutmeg
1 teaspoon ground cardamom

FOR THE PASTRY DOUGH

4 cups uncooked farina
½ pound (2 sticks) unsalted
   butter
¼ teaspoon kosher salt
1 cup plus 2 tablespoons
   rose water

FOR THE RICE FLOUR PASTRY

3 cups vegetable shortening
4⅓ cups rice flour
   (see Suppliers List, page 197)

This dish, in which a crunchy crust envelopes a smooth lentil mixture, is a classic Persian favorite.

For the dal, soak the lentils in 2 quarts of water for approximately 4 hours. Drain.

Add the lentils to 1 quart water in a large pot. Split the vanilla beans lengthwise and scrape the contents into the lentils. Add one of the split beans. Cook over a high flame until the lentils are soft, about 1 hour. (They should have dried out to a great extent.)

Add the sugar and stir until the mixture assumes a thick paste-like consistency. Remove the vanilla bean pieces. Mix in almonds, pistachios, cherries, nutmeg, and cardamom.

Remove the dal from the heat, divide into six balls, and set aside.

For the pastry dough, combine the farina, butter, salt, and rose water in the bowl of a standing mixer with a paddle attachment. Mix for about 3 minutes, until a dough forms.

Divide the dough into two balls, wrap in plastic, and refrigerate for 15 minutes.

{CONTINUED}

For the rice flour pastry, beat the shortening in the bowl of a standing mixer at medium speed with a paddle attachment until it becomes light and fluffy, about 7 minutes. Slowly add the rice flour and mix until incorporated.

Divide the dough into two balls, wrap in plastic, and refrigerate for 15 minutes.

Preheat the oven to 300° F. Spray a baking sheet with oil.

Roll out a ball of the pastry dough until it is a circle about a ¼ inch thick. Place one ball of the rice flour pastry on top and roll it out to match the size and shape. Sprinkle the dough with water and lightly dust with rice flour.

Roll up the pastry dough lengthwise and twist the roll three times to give it a cord-like appearance. Cut the roll into three equal pieces and twist each of these again. Shape each piece into a circle and flatten to 3 inches in diameter. Repeat with the remaining doughs. (You will have 6 circles.)

Place one of the circles in a small bowl and mold the dough to its concave form. Place a ball of dal in the center. Carefully fold over the sides of the dough, as if to form a dumpling. Wet the sides of the dough slightly if necessary to seal it. Remove from the bowl and flatten with the palm of your hand into a disc about ¾ inch thick. Repeat this procedure for the rest.

Place the discs on the baking sheet. Bake for approximately 30 minutes, turning them over halfway through the baking, until light gold. Serve at room temperature.

LENTILS are extremely high in protein, carbohydrates, and folic acid, and thus figure critically in the diet of vegetarian countries. India, for example, consumes more than half the world's lentils. This legume is part of the pea family but is more flattened in shape than most beans; in fact, the optic lens was named for the lentil (Latin: *lens*) because of its double convex shape. Lentils have been found in the tombs of the ancient Egyptians; and in the book of Genesis, Esau eats a plate of lentils just after giving up his birthright (in his memory, the French serve a lentil-based soup called potage Esau). Lentils appear in a variety of colors, including yellow, orange, black, brown, and green.

SUPPLEMENTAL RECIPES

Pepper-Coconut Sorbet

PLACE THE GELATIN SHEET in a bowl of cold water.

Combine 1 cup of the coconut puree and the pepper in a medium bowl and set aside.

In a saucepan, combine the remaining coconut puree with the sugar and bring to a simmer. Remove the gelatin from the water and wring out the excess liquid, as if from a towel. Add the gelatin to the warm coconut and whisk until completely dissolved. Mix into the reserved coconut puree.

Place in an ice bath to cool until syrupy.

Stir and process in an ice-cream machine, following the manufacturer's instructions, then put in the freezer until needed.

1 PINT

1 gelatin sheet (see Suppliers
  List, page 197)
2 cups frozen coconut puree,
  thawed (see Suppliers List,
  page 197)
3 turns of black pepper from a
  mill
½ cup sugar

Yuzu Sherbet

1 QUART

3 cups milk
½ cup sugar
1 cup yuzu juice (see Suppliers
    List, page 197)

IN A SMALL SAUCEPAN, whisk together the milk and sugar over a medium flame until the sugar is dissolved.

Remove from the heat and cool in an ice bath. Stir in the yuzu juice. Process in an ice-cream machine according to the manufacturer's instructions, then place in the freezer until needed

Brioche Dough

HEAT THE MILK until warm (95° F). Transfer to the bowl of a standing mixer. Stir in ½ teaspoon sugar and 1 tablespoon flour, crumble in the fresh yeast or sprinkle on the dry yeast, stir to blend, and cover. Set the bowl in a warm area for about 20 minutes.

Uncover the yeast mixture (which should be bubbling) and add the eggs and 1½ cups flour. Beat with a paddle attachment at medium speed for about 10 minutes, until the dough becomes sticky.

Add the butter, beat for another 5 minutes, and add the remaining sugar and the salt. Beat for another 3 minutes. Remove from the mixer.

Keeping the dough in the mixer bowl, spray the dough with a layer of oil. Then cover the bowl with plastic wrap and refrigerate for at least 4 hours, before use.

Remove the dough just before rolling.

If you want to make Brioche Buns, roll the dough into 2-ounce balls, spray with oil, and bake at 350° F till light golden in color.

 ½ SHEET TRAY

¼ cup milk
2 tablespoons plus ½ teaspoon sugar
2 cups plus 1 tablespoon all-purpose flour (½ cup of the flour will be used for dusting)
½ ounce fresh yeast or one ¼-ounce packet dry yeast
4 medium eggs
12 tablespoons (1½ sticks) unsalted butter, softened
½ teaspoon kosher salt

Strawberry Ice Cream

1 QUART

2 cups crushed fresh strawberries
(to get 2 cups of crushed strawberries, you will need about 3
cups of whole strawberries)
4 tablespoons strawberry liqueur
1 cup milk
1 cup heavy cream
¼ cup sugar
10 medium egg yolks

IN A SMALL BOWL, soak the strawberries in the liqueur.

Combine the milk, heavy cream and 2 tablespoons of the sugar in a medium saucepan and bring to a boil over a medium flame.

In the meanwhile, in a large bowl whisk together the egg yolks and the remaining 2 tablespoons sugar. Whisking continuously, add half the hot milk mixture to the egg yolks. Pour the yolk mixture back into the saucepan with the rest of the hot milk mixture and whisk together until well incorporated. Over a medium flame, continue to whisk for 30 seconds.

Remove from the heat and place the pan in an ice bath to cool.

Strain the cooled mixture through a fine sieve into a blender. Add the strawberries and puree.

Process in an ice-cream machine according to the manufacturer's instructions, then store in the freezer until needed.

Tart Shells

SIFT TOGETHER the pastry flour, almond flour, and salt into the bowl of a standing mixer. Add the butter and confectioners' sugar. Beat with a paddle attachment at low speed to add and blend in the ingredients; then beat at high speed for about 30 seconds, until the ingredients form a solid dough. Remove the dough from the mixer, form into a disc, wrap in plastic, and chill for at least 6 hours.

Preheat the oven to 325°F. Butter twelve 3-inch ring molds and place them on a baking sheet.

Roll out the dough on floured parchment paper into a thin sheet, and cut out circles according to size of the ring molds.

Place the circles in the pastry rings, lightly tamping down the center and edges, and rolling up the edges into a crust. Refrigerate for 10 minutes.

The dough will need to be weighed down during baking so that it stays flat; to do this, wrap uncooked beans or rice in small pieces of parchment paper, and place these in the center of the rings.

Bake the tart shells for 15 minutes. Remove the weights and bake another 3 to 5 minutes, until light gold. Cool to room temperature. Store in an airtight box until needed.

12 SHELLS

1½ cups pastry flour
½ cup almond flour
   (see Suppliers List, page 197)
1 teaspoon kosher salt
8 tablespoons (1 stick) unsalted
   butter, diced
1 cup confectioners' sugar

Selected Reading

BOOKS

Bakhru, H. K. *Indian Spices and Condiments as Natural Healers.* Mumbai: Jaico Publishing House, 2004.

Davidson, Frena Gray. *Ayurvedic Healing. Healing Wisdom.* Chicago: Keats Publishing, 2002.

Green, Aliza. *Field Guide to Herbs and Spices: How to Identify, Select, and Use Virtually Every Seasoning at the Market.* Philadelphia: Quirk Books, 2006.

———. *Field Guide to Produce: How to Identify, Select, and Prepare Virtually Every Fruit and Vegetable at the Market.* Philadelphia: Quirk Books, 2004.

Herbst, Sharon Tyler. *The New Food Lover's Companion: Comprehensive Definitions of Nearly 6,000 Food, Drink, and Culinary Terms.* 3rd ed. Hauppauge, NY: Barron's Educational Series, 2001.

Kowalchik, Claire, and William H. Hylton, eds. *Rodale's Illustrated Encyclopedia of Herbs.* Emmaus, PA: Rodale Press, 1987.

Lagassé, Paul, ed. *The Columbia Encyclopedia.* 6th ed. New York: Columbia University Press, 2000.

Sairam, T. V. *Home Remedies: A Handbook of Herbal Cures for Common Ailments.* New York: Penguin Books, 1998.

Toussaint-Samat, Maguelonne. Anthea Bell, trans. *A History of Food.* Cambridge, MA: Blackwell Reference, 1993.

ONLINE INFORMATION SOURCES

www.answers.com
www.bedemco.com
www.crfg.org/pubs/ff/
www.culinarycafe.com
www.epicureantable.com
www.etymonline.com/
www.foodreference.com/
www.globalherbalsupplies.com
www.health-care-clinic.org
www.herbalremedies.com
www.hort.purdue.edu/hort
www.innvista.com/HEALTH/foods/default.htm
www.mccormick.com/content.cfm?ID=8291
www.organic-planet.com/
www.theepicentre.com/
www.uni-graz.at/~katzer/engl/
www.vegparadise.com
www.whfoods.com/
www.wholehealthmd.com/

Suppliers List

ASIA MARKET CORPORATION

71½ Mulberry Street
New York, NY 10013
212-962-2020

Steamed buns

BROADWAY RESTAURANT SUPPLY

21 East 17th Street
New York, NY 10003
212-807-8877
www.broadwayrestaurantsupply.com

Kitchen supplies and equipment

JB PRINCE

36 East 31st Street N⁰11
New York, NY 10016
212-683-3553
800-473-0577
www.jbprince.com

Kitchen supplies and equipment

{CONTINUED}

KALUSTYAN'S
123 Lexington Avenue
New York, NY 10016
www.kalustyans.com
212-685-3451

Amchoor, asafetida, charoli nuts, clarified butter (ghee), goji berries, ground chicory, hibiscus flowers, kokum, Marcona almonds, orange oil, palmyra (palm fruit), verbena, yellow lentils, curry leaves, all spices, etc.

PARIS GOURMET
PO Box 12202
Newark, NJ 07101
www.parisgourmet.com

Almond paste, brik dough (pâte à brik), coconut puree, hazelnut paste, licorice powder, paillette feuilletine, pistachio oil, pistachio paste, raw chocolate (cocoa nibs), vanilla paste, gelatin sheets. This source sells mostly professional-size packages.

PORTO RICO IMPORTING COMPANY
201 Bleecker Street
New York, NY 10012
212-477-5421
800-453-5908
www.portorico.com

Ground chicory

Acknowledgments

NOTHING CAN BE ACHIEVED ALONE. TO GET ANYWHERE AT ANY point, one needs the whole package: love, strength, support, encouragement, razzle-dazzle, friendship, balance, luck, belief, validation, guidance, accessorization, courage, and at times even a fight. And sometimes one needs more than that: a tough wife to prod you on with promises of bliss when you finally get there. So, loads of love and thanks to my wife, Hinata.

For unconditional love and strength I have my mum; my dad; and my true friend, my sister Firoza, who is always there for me. For support I thank my entire extended family in India, especially my grandparents and the Kotak family.

There are a lot of others who have sharpened me into what I am today. Encouragement was offered by the most loyal and constant confidant, Andres Vazquez, who has been working with me for the last nine years. My staff, Mai Khanh Le, Emi Webster, Rajiv, and Christopher Anthony. My sincere friend and research guide Chris Kelly devoted hours to writing for me, and then more to listening over the phone. I am truly grateful to everyone at Sapa, especially Patricia Yeo, Gavin Portsmouth, and Brian Matzkow; to Dan Kluger of The Core Club; and to Philip Kirsh and Dan Levy at Aix. My absolutely amazing photographer Bill Durgin provided the razzle-dazzle with these stunning images.

Help and friendship have come in many ways, from listening to giving advice and support. Tom Lo, my loyal, brilliant, trusted friend, with whom I can share any secret. Didier Virot, whose sense of humor and friendship I value a lot, has made my years as a pastry chef very memorable. True friends—like Patience Kamen, who lays it out as it is,

Farhad, Kainaz, Sharon and Keoni Chang, and so many others–have always been there to provide balance.

Luck plays an important part in everyone's life. Sometimes one gets lucky by getting a great new contact; some days, a fantastic idea gets big. While that's all true, my luck extended to other areas too–I got a fabulous mother-in-law.

My sincere thanks to my publishers for recognizing my talent, believing in me, and then urging me to do more about it, especially Dan Halpern, Cassie Jones, Johnathan Wilber, Shubhani Sarkar, Millicent Bennett, and Richard Ljoenes.

Validation is the best form of respect, and I am extremely happy to have received it from some of the most talented people in my industry. When validation comes from food writers, it means the world. Eric Asimov, one of my favorite columnists, has been fabulous to me. Jim Curry, thanks for your continuous support. Thanks to Ruth Reichl for being the first to give me a write-up, and to Emily Prawda, Brooke Fitzsimmons, Mike Rucker, and Randall Lane for all your stuff in *Time Out*. Thanks to Karen Danick, director of media relations for *Gourmet*, for your useful chats, and to Andrea Strong for being there when needed. Thanks to Florence Fabricant for your encouragement, and of course Gael Green, William Grimes, Peter Meehan, and Frank Bruni for their views. Thank you to Pavia Rosati for your kind words in *Daily Candy*, and to Paul Andros of the *New York Sun*.

I received guidance at a tender age from my family and later from my peers Eric Hubert (my guru), Floyd Cardoz, Tony Liu, Mohan Ismail,

and Rocco DiSpirito. My sincere thanks to Jean-Georges Vongerichten for believing in me and inspiring me to get to the next level.

My work has been accessorized thanks to Steven Hall and Sam Frier, my publicists and confidants, who have done marvelous work with their team (Gael, Stephanie, Kyle, and Brian) over the years. Karen DiPerri, my thanks to you, too.

Finally, to succeed one sometimes needs to fight, and my wife, Hinata, showed me that by example. Her zest to fight and overcome breast cancer has been exemplary. Her strife taught me that one manages to muster more courage and work even harder when loved dearly–and a good fight does result in success.

Index

Page numbers in italic refer to photographs of prepared recipes.